The Other Daughters
of the Revolution

THE *other*

Daughters

OF THE

Revolution

The *Narrative* of K. White
{1809}

and the *Memoirs* of Elizabeth Fisher
{1810}

Edited and with an Introduction by

SHARON HALEVI

STATE UNIVERSITY OF NEW YORK PRESS

Published by
STATE UNIVERSITY OF NEW YORK PRESS
ALBANY

© 2006 State University of New York

For information, address
State University of New York Press
194 Washington Avenue, Suite 305, Albany, NY 12210-2384

Production, Laurie Searl
Marketing, Fran Keneston

Library of Congress Cataloging-in-Publication Data

The other daughters of the Revolution: The narrative of K. White and The memoirs of
Elizabeth Fisher/K. White, Elizabeth Fisher; edited and introduction by Sharon Halevi.
    p. cm.
    First work originally published: Schenectady : Printed for the authoress, 1809.
    Second work originally published: New York : Printed for the author, 1810.
    Includes bibliographical references and index.
    ISBN 0-7914-6817-8 (hardcover : alk. paper)
    1. White, K., b. 1772. 2. Fisher, Elizabeth Munro, b. 1759. 3. Women—United States—
Biography. 4. Women—United States—History—18th century. 5. Women—United
States—History—19th century. 6. Women—United States—Social conditions. 7. United
States—Biography. I. White, K., b. 1772. Narrative of the life, occurrences, vicissitudes and
present situation of K. White. II. Fisher, Elizabeth Munro, b. 1759. Memoirs of Mrs.
Elizabeth Fisher. III. Halevi, Sharon, 1958–

CT3260.O69 2006
973.3092'2—dc22
                                                                      2005025464

10   9   8   7   6   5   4   3   2   1

For my parents,
Sylvia and Samuel Ezekiel

Contents

Acknowledgments

It is always a pleasure to thank those who have supported and encouraged me in my work, especially this book, which took a long and at times winding path. I would particularly like to thank Mary-Jo Klein and Ellen Wurtzel of the Jay Papers Collection at Columbia University, who have the unenviable task of wading through the family papers, for answering my questions and pointing out items of particular interest to me. Mechal Sobel, Linda Kerber, Sheila Skemp, and several anonymous readers read earlier versions of this work and raised several issues I had not fully considered; I could not have hoped for a better group of commentators. My family probably ended up with more information on the lives of K. White and Elizabeth Fisher than they would have wished for in this lifetime; nevertheless, they bore my fascination with these two women with good humor. It is to them, especially my parents, I dedicate this work.

Introduction

In the early years of the nineteenth century two fascinating American women, K. White and Elizabeth Fisher, published autobiographical accounts of their lives. Like scores of other women and men in postrevolutionary America, White and Fisher sought to become the "heroes of their own lives."[1] By refashioning the events of their lives and presenting their version of their trials and tribulations to an avid readership, the two sought to wrest at least symbolic control over their lives and identities and to reassert their independence. Neither elite nor even middle class, the two women, who existed on the margins of their society, illuminate through their writings popular attitudes toward women, marriage, and a set of emerging dominant ideologies.

The stories K. White and Elizabeth Fisher told correspond to each other on several key points (time period, biography, location, and ideology), each complementing the other's historical basis and the veracity of their sentiments. Of the two texts, Fisher's *Memoirs* is plainer, in terms of style and rhetoric; nevertheless it is a compelling account of a woman's life and struggles during and after the revolutionary period. Fisher's *Memoirs* enables the reader to situate her as a historically verifiable character; in fact, she made a point of providing her prospective reader with specific details (names, dates, places) to bolster her claims—legal claims, as the reader finds out in the closing pages of the *Memoirs*. In contrast, in her *Narrative*, K. White went to considerable lengths to obscure her identity, leaving the authorship of the more sophisticated text open to speculation. It is possible that the text was written by a "real" woman writing a basically true account of her life, a female author writing a fictional account, or a male author writing a fictional account (nevertheless, I will refer to White as "she" throughout this essay).[2]

The lives of the two women ran along parallel courses. Both were the daughters of Scottish immigrants to the American colonies. The two women underwent traumatic periods in their childhood. Both were the daughters of loyalists and due to their families' decision to remain loyal to the British crown during the Revolutionary War, the two were separated from their families and their homes. Despite this they retained their ties to the United States. Eventually, both women found themselves entangled in unhappy marriages. Abandoned for extended periods, they were forced to take on the role of sole provider. Later they became embroiled in property disputes with their male kin, which eventually landed them in prison (where they began writing their narratives).

Elizabeth Munro Fisher (1759–1845) was born in Pennsylvania. Her father, Henry Munro, was serving as a chaplain in the British army, when he met and married Elizabeth's mother, who was the widow of one of his fellow officers. Both her mother and her first stepmother died soon after childbirth and Elizabeth spent several years with a nurse, until her father's remarriage in 1766 to Eve Jay, the eldest daughter of the prominent New York family. Fisher suffered years of verbal and physical abuse by her stepmother, and eventually convinced her father to permit her to live apart from the family. When her father decided to marry her off without her consent, she married Donald Fisher against her father's wishes. The couple and their son lived near Albany until the outbreak of the Revolution, when the family's loyalist sympathies forced them to leave the area and relocate to Montreal. Elizabeth Fisher and her husband, spent several years in Canada, where she gave birth to four more children. Fisher and her family eventually returned to upstate New York, although Elizabeth and her husband had begun to live separately since 1791. From 1800 onward, Elizabeth was embroiled in lengthy legal battle with her half-brother, Peter Jay Munro, over two thousand acres of land, which both claimed as their inheritance. When attempts to settle the matter out of court failed, Elizabeth was brought up on charges of forgery, convicted, and sentenced to prison in New York City. In 1806 she was released from prison and lived in New York City for the next four years; it was during this period that she began writing her *Memoirs*.

K. White (1772–?) was born in Scotland, arrived in the colonies as a young child, and settled with her parents in Boston. After the outbreak of the Revolution, White was sent to school in Stockbridge. A few months later, she was captured by the Indians; White endured several months in captivity until she escaped and was reunited with her parents. At the age of seventeen White was engaged to marry a young American officer; a few days before their wedding he committed suicide and much to White's dismay she learned that he was already married. Soon after this, White caved in to family pressure and married S. White, who soon abandoned her pregnant and saddled with debt, after he had seduced their maid. In an attempt to provide for herself, White became a merchant; troubles with her husband's creditor landed her in court and eventually forced her out of Boston. Over the next few years, she moved from one place to another in upstate New York, relishing the predicaments her gender-ambiguous appearance landed her in; she settled eventually in Albany, where she began to write her *Narrative*.

The lives of the two women indicate that the postrevolutionary and early national periods were tumultuous ones, both in political and personal terms. They were periods of self-invention and renegotiation, witnessing the reformulation of core, fundamental relationships: those between the mother country and her former colony, between the state and its citizens, between the free and the enslaved, between men and women, and between husbands and wives. Western political theory, which had long employed the family and family relationships as an allegory for the state and the state's relationship with its subjects or citizens, could no longer escape the personal implications of the political changes ushered by the American Revolution. The intense intellectual work of renegotiating these relationships and of forging a new self-identity (be it of the nation or its individual citizens) often took literary form, especially fictional and nonfictional narratives of self. These narratives trace the outlines of what Cathy Davidson has called a "symbolic map" of the mentalités of the early Republic (1993, 287), and K. White and Elizabeth Fisher in their provocative and invaluable tales provide many of the details of this map. Similar to other women's autobiographies published in this period, White's and Fisher's narratives of self present an unruly, disobedient, and assertive female subject. By articulating a consistent and growing unease concerning the institution of marriage and the unlimited power husbands had over their wives, this genre was laying the groundwork for a political critique of marriage and the status of married women within it.

In the course of their lives K. White and Elizabeth Fisher witnessed both a major political transformation and the onset of an economic transformation, which would reach its peak in the nineteenth century. These changes ushered in a set of new gender ideologies. Women were expected to adhere, display, and foster republican virtues, but they were increasingly expected to withdraw from any involvement in political and public affairs and content themselves with the smooth running of their families and households. Linda Kerber has argued that only by adopting the model of the "Republican mother" and placing their intellects and skills in the service of their families could women hope to reconcile these two conflicting demands and avoid public censure (Kerber [1980] 1986).

Several women's historians have since continued tracing the impact of the role of the "Republican mother." While the model of female republican virtue (which included characteristics such as self-reliance, industriousness, sacrifice, self-discipline, benevolence, frugality, and patriotism) was certainly different from that expected of males, both were seen as necessary for the continued welfare of the new nation. The mother, who faithfully inculcated these values to her sons and daughters and wielded moral authority over her husband, provided an invaluable service both to her family and to her country (Bloch 1987; Zagarri 1992). The republican marriage, a union of "like-minded and virtuous men and women" bound together by affection, would ensure the happiness and continued prosperity of the couple and the nation (Lewis 1987, 720). However, beneath this optimistic rhetoric lurked a grim reality, for "affectionate marriage, a hallmark of republican political rhetoric, obscures the violation of democratic principles" when the wife's legal and political identity becomes subsumed in that of her husband (Barnes 1997, 11). Shirley Samuels argues that fiction played an important role in promoting this ideal of republican marital bliss. "Postulating the happy family operates to keep citizens in line with the state as well as to buffer the sensation of state control, and fiction provides the clearest expression of that family" (Samuels 1996, 19).

The concepts of republican virtue, as familiar to White and Fisher as to other sons and daughters of the Revolution, were being feminized by the turn of the eighteenth century. Ruth Bloch attributes these changes to new meanings of virtue generated by evangelical Christianity, Lockean psychology, and literary sentimentalism (Bloch 1987). Women's historians of the mid-1960s argued that as the workplace moved outside the home in the course of the nineteenth century, there appeared an increasing rhetorical separation of men and women's spheres of activity. The ideology of "separate spheres" naturalized this rhetorical separation between public and private, political and personal. As women were deemed physically weaker, but morally superior to men, they were best suited to the domestic sphere. There they were expected to embody the feminine virtues of piety, purity, submissiveness, and domesticity (Lerner 1969; Welter 1966).

Later historians and literary critics challenged these views, stressing that the dominant gender ideologies were not seamless; in fact they were rife with tensions, contradictions, and ambivalence. While they retained much of their persuasive powers during the years following the American Revolution their impact on different groups of women was uneven. For example, while many women came to recognize "separate spheres" as an ideology that provided them with an alternative source of power and the basis for the establishment of a female community (Cott 1977; Smith-Rosenberg 1975), others, such as working-class women, immigrant women, rural women, and especially black women (both enslaved and free), found that their exclusion from this paradigm (because of their "failure" to be pious and "pure") made them vulnerable to physical and psychological abuse (Kelley 2001). Both historians and literary critics recognize that these dominant gender ideologies were often prescriptive rather than descriptive, and that by themselves they are inadequate to explain the lived experience of women in the early republican and antebellum periods (Davidson 1998; Kerber 1988).

The work of anthropologist James Scott offers one way of connecting the prescriptive ideologies with lived experience. Scott has argued that social discourses range from the side of the subordinate discourse in the presence of the dominant ("the public transcript"), to a discourse concealed from the eyes of the dominant ("the hidden transcript"). As the dominant group in the Early Republic consisted mostly of white, middle- and upper-class, men (and to a lesser extent women), other groups, be they immigrants or working-class people, free and enslaved blacks, or women from all walks of life, were forced to concede to the dominant group's political and cultural hegemony, to mask their restlessness and obscure their criticism. This hidden transcript includes all those "speeches, gestures, and practices that confirm, contradict, or inflect what appears in the public transcript" (Scott 1990, 4–5). In the South for example, free and enslaved blacks met secretly in secluded areas or in the slave quarters and conspired to rebel openly against their masters ("the hidden transcript"); they also told trickster tales. Using metaphors, allusions, and stock characters, such as Brer Rabbit and John and Old Master, they veiled their hatred of slavery by producing a seemingly innocuous oral tradition ("the public transcript"), which could be retold even in the presence of their masters. Thus, having grasped the price of open, public insubordination, subordinates learned to conceal their discontent and criticism from the eyes of the dominant—so much so that they are often seen as complicit in contributing to a sanitized official transcript.

I suggest that a similar development occurred with women's texts. Women's novels, which appealed to a middle- and upper-class audience, were more likely to mask open expressions of dissatisfaction, while the narratives of self appearing in the cheap and ephemeral pamphlets were more likely to voice them. Scott's insights make it possible to sift the prescriptive from the descriptive in these two narratives of self; they enable readers to understand why White and Fisher each chose to frame her life as she did, and to discern the relationship between the two transcripts. It is this awareness of the gaps and contradictions between "public and hidden transcripts" and the social forces that necessitate the adoption of the "public transcript," that readers must bring to their reading and analysis of K. White's and Elizabeth Fisher's texts.

Felicity Nussbaum formulates a similar argument regarding autobiographical writing, although she frames it in different terms. She claims that "autobiographical writing allows the previously illiterate and disenfranchised to adopt a language sufficiently acceptable to be published, and, at the same time, it enables them to envisage new possibilities in the interstices between discourses or to weave them together in new hybrid forms" (Nussbaum 1989, 37). Nussbaum argues that while narratives of self produce, reproduce, confirm, and undermine prevailing ideologies of perceiving and representing reality, in their private forms (i.e., those not intended for publication) they often reinscribe these ideologies. While individuals may identify with these ideologies, they themselves or others may also fully or partially reject them,[3] thereby revealing previously invisible aspects of these ideologies. It is at this point that individuals may be able to create new subject positions, through which change may be effected. White and Fisher not only wrote as women but they focused their narratives on their experiences as married women. Nussbaum's argument suggests that they (like other married women in the period) took seriously the models of the "republican mother" or the "republican marriage," but were on some other levels quite critical of it.

Novels have held a special place in the lives of American women, for more than any other literary and cultural form they were "dedicated to the proposition that women's experience was worthy of detailed, sympathetic, and thoughtful attention" (Davidson 1993, 286). Situated, as the novels' plots were, within the events of women's lives, the novels presented their readers alternative scenarios of what life as a woman might hold in store for them. Linda Kerber argues that the numerous attacks on women's choice of reading material, especially the novels, should be viewed in a large part as attacks on emotion, passion, and sexuality. Critics feared that novel reading, both as a solitary interpretive activity and as a fictional confession of a secret, hidden, or private self, would foster a view of the self as the ultimate source of authority, and thus would encourage independence and other inappropriate forms of female behavior (Kerber [1980] 1986, 241–45).

Critique of the novel in America peaked after the Revolution, just as issues such as authority, personal and political liberty, and the limits of the pursuit of happiness were being debated as well. Critics of the novel in the early nineteenth century were well aware of the threat it presented. The novel was a subversive genre, because it destabilized notions of form, style, and subject matter. But just as disturbing as its choice of characters and plots was its intended audience: a popular audience, made up of both sexes and all classes, which needed to possess only a basic education in order to read the novel unsupervised. Women in particular became the focus of the critics' diatribes. Despite the numerous denunciations in the press, sermons, advice books, and surprisingly enough in novels themselves, the readership of the novels grew, first and foremost through the increase in the numbers of circulating libraries. By midcentury, when novels became less expensive, their readers began to buy and own them, reading them devotedly time and again (Davidson 1993).

One of the main differences between political tracts and novels was that, while the political rhetoric of the period utilized the "disembodied unspecific male" to stand in for both the individual and the collective, sentimental fiction worked out sociopolitical questions on a gendered body. As a result "the woman's body serves as a synecdoche for the emotional susceptibility of the republic" (Barnes 1997, 8). Although the inner working of a marriage and power relations within the family were the focal point of both novels and more popular and cheaper pamphlets, the pamphlets expressed significantly greater ambivalence and unease with the institution and contained a far more subversive subtext. While in political tracts and sentimental novels "Republican Motherhood," companionate marriages, and the joys of domesticity were often lauded as highly desirable ideals, the fictional and nonfictional female narratives of self found in pamphlets not only noted the flaws and failures of these ideals, but launched a sustained critique of the institution of marriage and the position of women within it. These two distinct, but interconnected, literary styles were part of an ongoing discourse on women, and wives in particular. However, this discourse was not monolithic, it ranged over an entire spectrum; authors drew upon a shared set of values, images, and texts, but differed in their responses to them.

The early nineteenth century witnessed the emergence of a distinct women's genre in pamphlet form, tales of marital and domestic discord. The authors drew upon a long-standing Anglo-American popular literary tradition, which focused on disorder, abuse, and violence within the family (Dolan 1994; Kane 1996; Robb 1997). Although the novels of this period (which expressed more of the "public transcript") have been extensively analyzed, and historians have recently turned their attention to women's magazines of the period (Aronson 2002; List 1994), far less attention has been paid to the personal, fictional and nonfictional, narratives published in the pamphlets (which incorporated more of the "hidden transcript").[4] When researchers have turned their attention to pamphlets, they have focused on the numerous ones of the antebellum period and especially on sensationalist fiction and nonfiction (Branson 1996; Keetley 1998, 1999).

The narratives of K. White and Elizabeth Fisher are part of a much larger (albeit ephemeral) body of pamphlet literature written by women during the early nineteenth century. The texts that have survived tell a perturbing tale of women's lives during this period. Abigail Abbot Bailey, for example, told the story of her twenty-five year marriage to an abusive, violent, and adulterous husband, whom she eventually divorced in 1793 only after he had sexually abused one of their daughters (Taves 1989). Eliza Ann Alby recounted the tale of her numerous pre- and extramarital affairs and her abandonment of her six children (1840?). Ellen Stephens told of her husband's abandonment. Left with their infant child, Stephens masquerades as a young man and goes in search of her husband, working as a cabin boy on a Mississippi steamboat (1840). Elizabeth Hill narrated her history of parental abuse, early widowhood and the economic difficulties facing a single mother struggling to survive and provide for her children (Hill 1852).

Ostensibly this literature was intended as a caution to its readers, but its entertainment value was high as well; bookstores and lending libraries stocked up on this relatively inexpensive literary genre. Fictional tales and nonfictional narratives of self written by or about abandoned women, abused wives who then murdered their husbands, unfaithful or bigamous wives, poisoners, and female criminals (often those awaiting execution)

made up the staple fare of these pamphlets. Many of the later fictional sensationalist tales consciously took on the form of a narrative of self (memoirs, journals, letters, and autobiographies). These pamphlets explored the
inner workings of a marriage that had possessed the capacity to turn a virtuous married woman into a murderer, and an intemperate man into an
abuser. The themes and issues present in these pamphlets run counter to
the dominant discourses of "Republican Motherhood," domesticity, and
the ideology of "separate spheres."

While great consideration has been given to the dominant ideologies
articulated in the novels, and the ways they shaped an evolving transat-
lantic feminist consciousness, less attention has been focused on the oppo-
sitional ideologies found in the pamphlets. Both are the precursors of a
feminist consciousness, which would emerge in political form in the mid-
nineteenth century. A growing number of literary critics and historians
have been voicing similar views. Cathy Davidson and Laura McCall have
ably demonstrated that the domestic novels themselves can be viewed as
a subversive genre. Davidson argues that even novelists, who expressed
much more traditional, perhaps even reactionary, views regarding marriage and the appropriate role of a wife, such as Helena Wells in her novel
Constantia Neville (1800) and S. S. B. K. Wood in *Amelia* (1802), under-
mined the "public transcript" by presenting a dreary and bleak picture of
what happens to the women who adhered to it (Davidson 1998). McCall,
who conducted a content and textual analysis of best-selling novels and
stories published between 1820 and 1860, found that "obedient and
dependent women were not the ideal in either men's or women's fiction"
(McCall 2001, 98). Even when these novels lauded marriage as a woman's
highest aspiration, they put forth alternatives to marriage and portrayed
women achieving objectives outside marriage. McCall's findings echo
those of earlier studies; Nina Baym, for example, argues that these novels
very often posited an individualistic and self-assured heroine and that they
articulated a form of "a moderate, or limited, or pragmatic feminism"
(Baym 1984, 18; see also Kelley 1984).

Because of the long-standing tradition of equating the state and its
relationship with its subjects or citizens to the family or marriage and the
emotional bonds that sustain them, fiction (in book or pamphlet form) and
narratives of self dealing with family and marital relations were, by any
standard, political statements. They constitute an integral part of the political discourse of the early Republic. The particular conventions of each
genre enabled authors to articulate elements of the "hidden transcript," to

put forward their own answers to political and social questions, which might have encountered far greater resistance had they appeared in other literary forms. Because the novels could be labeled as fictional and the narratives of self as personal, and therefore nonrepresentative, the political critique they represented could be contained and tolerated.[5] Thus it is possible that early-nineteenth-century readers read the breakdown of White's and Fisher's respective marriages, and in fact their inability to sustain any kind of family ties, as symbolic of the failure and collapse of the old political order, and the loyalist cause in particular. They could also have concluded that in a world that saw the disintegration of the colonial relationship between "Mother" England and her unruly daughter, America, other familial relationships were rendered vulnerable. But the threat and fear some readers may have felt in face of these unruly narratives of self may have also led them to read these two accounts (and others like them) as merely the out of the ordinary tales of two unhappy, marginal women.

White's and Fisher's narratives present unrelenting tales of betrayal and abuse, especially by the people who were supposed to protect them. Both women were abandoned by their parents, both literally and symbolically. Fisher's mother died a few days after giving birth to her, and Elizabeth was sent off to live with a nurse while her father served as chaplain with his regiment. When she was three years old, her father remarried, but less than a year later her beloved first stepmother died soon after she gave birth to a baby. After her stepmother's death, Fisher's father once again placed her and her half-brother (who soon died as well) in the care of the nurse, while he left for England. Upon her father's remarriage a few years later to Eve Jay (his third wife), Elizabeth was taken once again from her nurse and placed in the care of her stepmother, while her father set off on his ministry once again. According to Fisher, Eve Jay Munro abused her and her half-brother, Peter Jay Munro, both verbally and physically. Eight-year-old K. White was sent away to school in Stockbridge after the outbreak of the Revolution, when her loyalist father left Boston for England, leaving the family behind. White was soon taken captive by Indians and spent several months with them before escaping.

Some of these events were clearly not within the control of the two girls' parents, and the parents, especially their fathers, responded to these events in a manner most contemporaries would have found reasonable. K. White's parents may have wished to keep her out of harm's way and spare her the public abuse heaped on loyalists and their families. Henry Munro, who was himself recovering from the deaths of two wives and an infant son, was trying to advance himself in the world and contract an advantageous marriage alliance, which he did by marrying into the prominent Jay family. Once he did, he immediately placed his daughter in his new wife's care. Yet, it is difficult not to sympathize with two very young girls and their pain, which are obvious years after the events took place. What was clearly not acceptable to Elizabeth, nor the servants and neighbors for that matter, was Munro's neglect of his daughter's physical and emotional welfare. Fisher acknowledged that it was the kindness of strangers, the servants who slipped her food and the interference of the neighbors who informed her father of her continued abuse, which enabled her to survive those traumatic years (though with deep emotional scars). In view of her childhood experiences, Elizabeth Fisher's inability to trust, or to form lasting emotional attachments with people, is not surprising.

K. White preceded her captivity narrative with a statement claiming that her parents were loving and affectionate. This is only one of two cases she admits these feelings toward anyone in the course of her tale. White mentions her father only once again in the *Narrative*, in the course of a following chapter, when she recounts his insistence that she marry S. White, her future husband, who deserted her. Twice, although well intentioned, her father had failed to protect her.

Their fathers' role in arranging their marriages was a sore point for both women. Although both women stressed their right to marry for love, rather than for economic considerations or parental pressure, they did not do so. As a result they did ascribe (perhaps unconsciously) part of the blame for the failure of their marriages to their respective fathers. White claimed that her father did not recognize duplicity of her first suitor, a bigamist who committed suicide before the wedding, or the perfidy of the second, who would become her future husband. Fisher's father insisted she marry a man more than twenty years her senior with whom she was barely acquainted. Munro's attempt to arrange unilaterally his daughter's marriage ran counter to what was the accepted norm in America. By this time young men and women selected their future spouses, while their parents retained at best veto power over their decisions (Shumsky 1976; Whyte 1992). When Fisher refused to accede to her father's choice and in a desperate act of defiance chose a few months later to marry Donald Fisher (a man she did not love), her father disinherited her.

White claimed that she had barely recovered from the "melancholy" she lapsed into following her fiancé's death, when she yielded to her father who "was strenuous to win my consent to a union with S- W-" (*Narrative*, 43).

Fisher reconstructed for her readers her thoughts at the time of her marriage: "I shall have someone to take care of me—I shall have a home—I shall never be a trouble to my father . . . and another thing which had great weight on my mind, was, that I should be out of my stepmother's power" (*Memoirs*, 81). By failing to recognize their daughters' needs, fears, and desires both fathers pushed their daughters into unhappy and miserable marriages.

Both marriages soured after a few months. Within a year of their marriage, after impregnating their maid, White's husband deserted her. White, who was also with child, was left to deal with the social and economic consequences of this desertion. Although Elizabeth Fisher did admit that her husband was "fond" of her, she became so despondent in the months following her marriage that at one point she seriously contemplated suicide.

White and Fisher were highly critical of the legal and political system, which placed them under the power of their male relatives, especially their husbands. The middle-class social expectation, that they remain emotionally and economically dependent, compelled them to marry, but once married they were denied both companionship and financial security. Both women disparaged their respective husbands' economic ineptitude. White, in particular, made the connection between the personal and the political; her husband's failure to provide for her became emblematic of the financial power husbands wielded over their wives. "Too many females," she observed, "are lost to society by the inattention and cruelty of their husbands, who, instead of benevolently aiding and giving them comfort, consign them to the bitter cup of poverty and distress. How many vices and crimes owe their birth to these causes!" (*Narrative*, 63).

Their husbands' inability to provide for them, and in Elizabeth Fisher's case her husband's political loyalties, left both women socially and economically vulnerable. The two women's attempts to recover their finances, their entanglements with their creditors and the law, and their respective husbands' attempts to reassert financial control over them, make up the bulk of their remaining stories. If, as Lenore Davidoff and Catherine Hall argue, female gentility was increasingly associated with not only a withdrawal from the public sphere, but with a reluctance to act as a "visibly economic agent" (1987, 315), then both White and Fisher rejected, if only due to economic necessity, this form of bourgeois femininity offered for their emulation. Both actively asserted their right to engage in financial transactions, to own property, and to dispose of it according to their own will, while their husbands attempted to force them back into economic dependence.

Despite their rejection of an emerging dominant model of middle-class, white femininity, Fisher and White often seem to measure their lives against that standard. Time and again they interjected their narratives with asides to their readers, which suggest that they were unwittingly reevaluating their lives against those norms. These asides are also some of the best examples of how White and Fisher are complicit in producing a sanitized official transcript. Fisher went to great lengths to explain her estrangement from her husband by stressing how time and again he promised to provide for her; when she relented and went to live with him, it became clear he had had no intention of keeping his promises. He took all their money and left for England and then the United States, leaving her and their children without any funds to support themselves. Later, after once again failing to provide his family with a home, Fisher's husband and his natal family confiscated all of Elizabeth's possessions in order to prevent her from returning with the children to Canada (*Memoirs*, 89).

Fisher explains her independent and unsubmissive behavior then, not by asserting her right to do so, but by proving her husband's ineptness as a husband and a provider. Yet at the same time she is rejecting her prescribed role as a wife, she is confirming it. A few pages later, she tells of her husband's death and notes, "[A]fter his death I seemed to be more reconciled, for he was a great trouble to me when living" (*Memoirs*, 90). Immediately, as if she herself were startled and uncomfortable with her statement, which ran counter to any bourgeois notion of a companionate marriage, she attempts to justify her blunt sentiments by establishing his disregard for her feelings and relating how in an act of vindictiveness he sold her enslaved woman, who had probably been her sole emotional support during these trying years (*Memoirs*, 90).

Fisher had also internalized the middle-class notions of a companionate marriage, although she was well aware of the fact that both her marriage and her father's marriage to Eve Jay failed to adhere to this ideal. She meticulously noted the symptoms of this marital failure: separate beds, constant fights and disagreements, threats, and prolonged absences. She was also aware that her emotions toward and relationship with her parents did not conform to middle-class expectations of a parent-child relationship. Her feelings toward her father were ambivalent at best even toward the end of her account (*Memoirs*, 100). While she was unable to reconcile or even express feelings of anger and resentment toward her father, she was more than able to articulate them toward her stepmother, and during her childhood often found animal surrogates and acted out her violent emotions on them. In a manner reminiscent of the eighteenth-century Parisian artisans, who massacred their masters' cats (Darnton 1984), Fisher vented her hatred of her stepmother and the anger she felt at the stepmother's mistreatment of her onto the favored household pets, poisoning, drowning, and slaughtering them (*Memoirs*, 93–95).[6] Fisher was fully aware that these acts not only upset her stepmother and preyed on her anxieties, but also were sure to increase the tensions between her and Henry Munro, as her stepmother inevitably vented her anger onto him.

Later in the *Memoirs* Fisher must come to terms with her "failure" as a mother, not so much because she failed to care and provide for her children (the requirement of a working-class mother) but because of her failure to establish and foster long-lasting emotional bonds with them (the requirement of a middle-class mother). Fisher projected onto her children her sense of failure to maintain the mother-child emotional bond, accusing them of neglecting her because of her poverty. She attempted to enlist her readers' sympathies by requesting those who are parents to place themselves in her shoes, and asked: "Can children, let them be ever so kind, repay their mother for what she has to undergo in body and in mind, in bringing them up till they are able to do for themselves? I say they cannot" (*Memoirs*, 102).

White made similar comparisons to an emerging sex/gender system when forced to explain her gender transgressions, as a cross-dresser, as a woman who made sexual advances toward other women, and as a woman who defined her honor in masculine terms.[7] The main purpose of a sex/gender system is to define the sociopolitical boundaries between different human bodies and check any violations. These violations do not necessarily arouse anxiety and horror; in fact they may prove to be sources of pleasure and excitement. In the eighteenth century when the popularity of the tales of such (real and fictional) gender transgressors, in particular masquerading heroines, peaked, they were a source of pleasure. However, by the early nineteenth century as their popularity declined they were increasingly becoming a source of concern and even panic (Cressy 1996; Dekker and van der Pol 1989; Dugaw 1989; Wharman 1998). While the tales of these gender transgressive women (whether transvestites, confidence women, or spies) never completely disappeared during the course of the nineteenth century, they were most certainly muted (De Grave 1995).

White's explanations of her disorderly behavior, as a woman who made a play for other women, were designed to neutralize her readers' growing hostility to it, by admitting to the events and appealing to her readers' indulgence, terming one of these transgressions as "a freak of the moment which my better judgment wholly condemned" (*Narrative*, 48), and another as a "foolish adventure" (*Narrative*, 59). By framing these incidents as aberrations or jokes and recognizing their impropriety, White defuses their subversive potential, producing yet again a more sanitized transcript.

A few chapters later the unrepentant White is right back at it, this time claming for herself not the appearance or sexual prerogatives of a man, but her right to a masculine definition of her honor. White rejected the prevailing view regarding female honor, which was predicated upon a woman's sexual behavior and reputation. According to this view, insults could only detract from a woman's honor and her male kin (as the ones most affected by these insults) were responsible for seeking redress. While men were not invulnerable to sexual insult, their honor was not predicated solely upon their sexual behavior; they were also able to accrue honor through acts of bravery or the fulfillment of civic duty (Gowing 1993; Norton 1987).

Again it is useful to compare the responses of Elizabeth Fisher and K. White to attacks on their honor. In 1789 (after living apart for several years) Donald Fisher suspected Elizabeth Fisher of having "criminal connexion" with a young lodger (*Memoirs*, 95). At the instigation of Donald Fisher's nephew, the young man was brought before a justice, examined, and released on his oath, but Elizabeth's reputation was irrevocably and very publicly tarnished. While Fisher was furious with her husband's behavior, she did not say one word during these public proceedings; only in the privacy of his house did she challenge and taunt him. In contrast, White behaved as a man would: seeking redress for her honor and contrasting her bravery with the cowardly behavior of her male opponents. In the first instance, her irate landlord, who had believed she was man in female disguise, verbally abused White for spending time in private with his wife. White responded by presenting him with her brace of pistols, and reasoned "as he judged me to be a man I would act up to it"; her landlord hastily declined the offer to duel (*Narrative*, 59). In the next town, White was suspected of being a British spy. She soon challenged to a duel the young man suspected of spreading these rumors. Only when the young man realized she was serious about carrying out her challenge did he agree to retract his charges (*Narrative*, 61–63).[8]

Regenia Gagnier argues that this pattern of rejection mixed with acceptance of middle-class gender ideology often appeared in the autobiographical writings of nineteenth-century working-class men and women who, in an attempt to analyze their lives through narrative, adopted literary models derived from the writings of middle-class authors, models that reflected the realities of a bourgeois life. "However," she claims, "their experience cannot be analyzed in terms of their acculturation" (1991, 46). The ensuing gap between ideology and experience exacted a very high psychic cost from the women and men who did not lead a bourgeois life, and the result is not only the disintegration of the narrative, but also, Gagnier argues, the disintegration of the personality itself. Stephen Arch also senses this disintegration, and as a result concludes that "White's and Fisher's narratives are not fully emerged as autobiographies" (2001, 156).

Fisher and White did indeed present fragmented narratives and selves. They proposed to tell the story of their lives in coherent and more or less chronological order but they did not do so. Feminist scholars have noted that fragmented selves, spaces in the narrative, temporal shifts, are characteristic of women's narratives of self (Smith and Watson 1998; Benstock 1998). The two narratives contain large gaps (an issue I will return to near the end of the last section). Fisher's narrative is interspersed by "flashbacks" to her childhood, while White mixes genres as easily as she blends genders.

GENDER AND GENRE

White's and Fisher's narratives of self, like other such narratives, which appeared in pamphlet or in book form, were intimately connected to the early novel which often took the guise of a narrative of self (letters, diary, memoirs) to gain authority and veracity. As noted earlier, the two texts echo each other on several important points (time period, biography, location, and ideology), each reinforcing the other's historical basis and the authenticity of opinions expressed. However, there are also significant differences between the two texts.

Fisher's *Memoirs* is a fairly straightforward text, written in simple prose. It contains very few literary allusions, and but for a few flashbacks and flash-forwards, it is organized according to a linear timeline, beginning with her parents' acquaintance and ending with a description of Fisher's life after her release from prison. White's *Narrative*, on the other hand, is a highly crafted text, almost an embryonic or proto-novel, which incorporates several separate subgenres (the captivity narrative, the seduction tale, the narrative of marital woes, the cross-dressing narrative, and the prison account) and interweaves poetry and prose. The text may be read as an early draft version of a picaresque novel, one in which White is experimenting with various literary genres, testing their suitability, attempting to fit the square pegs of episodes in her life into the round holes of preexisting genres. Yet, if read as a whole the use of these subgenres further destabilizes and subverts the coherency of the narrative and the woman who is its subject. The reader is never afforded the luxury of comfort, a sensation that accompanies any reader familiar with the conventions of a particular literary genre chosen by the author. White constantly pulls the rug from under the reader's feet; just as the reader is about to settle comfortably into the conventions of the captivity narrative, White shifts to the narrative of seduction, only to shift a few pages later to the story of a female transvestite. These constant shifts between literary genres, poetry and prose, references to texts outside her text, and allusions to duplicitous or Janus-faced mythological and mythic characters (such as Hymen, Mercury, Fortune, or Pope Joan); constantly reemphasize the overall quality of destabilization and subversion.

The first subgenre to make its appearance in White's *Narrative* is the captivity narrative. Captivity narratives were the most popular literary genre during the colonial period and their popularity endured well into the nineteenth century. They played an important role in the formation of an American national identity by testing the boundaries of racial and gender identity (Smith-Rosenberg 1993). These narratives (especially the ones written by women) had a strong influence on the evolution of sentimental fiction on both sides of the Atlantic (Armstrong 1998). They posited a new kind of female heroine, who through her moral fortitude and courage, rejected a more stereotypical definition of femininity and the conventions of domesticity and redefined feminine virtue. White's sketchy account of her Indian captivity ends abruptly with her midnight escape and her joyous reunion with her family. She skipped over the events in her life during the following years and resumed the story of her life at the age of seventeen, with the no less popular seduction narrative.

Seduction was a theme seriously and regularly explored in popular novels and periodical literature of the late eighteenth century and by the early years of the nineteenth it began to be presented on stage. One of the more notable and highly popular articulations of this theme in America was Susanna Rowson's *Charlotte Temple* (1791), which tells the story of a young English girl who elopes to America with her seducer. There she is abandoned and dies soon after giving birth to her daughter. Some historians view the increased usage of the seduction theme as a form of cultural backlash against the growing independence of young adults from patriarchal control, especially when it came to marital choices (Hessinger 1998). By casting young men in the role of unrestrained predators, the authors were able to impress upon young women the necessity of placing themselves voluntarily under benign parental supervision.

White's account of her first courtship and engagement conforms to the conventions of the seduction tale. She fell in love with a young army officer; the two were soon engaged and began preparations for their marriage. A few days before the wedding, her fiancé left Boston abruptly and soon after his return committed suicide. The details of this tale conform, step by step, to the conventions of the genre. Her fiancé is a would-be bigamist, who in true literary fashion repents before the wedding, confessing in a letter to his first marriage and his undying love and respect for White, and then obligingly commits suicide.

Next, the readers were introduced to a tale of marital woes. Elizabeth Barnes has argued that although seduction and marriage have been portrayed in fiction as "antithetical models of heterosexual relations," both symbolize the complex relationship between coercion and consent. Both represent a "relationship paradigm" based on an imbalance of power, which is rendered temporarily invisible by the language of affection (1997, 11). Both White and Fisher viewed this disparity of power as the source of their troubles; their inability to influence their husbands' political and economic choices and their initial ignorance of financial and legal matters left them vulnerable and hard-pressed to fend for themselves. Their accounts echo themes from sentimental fiction: the unfaithfulness of husbands, the emotional abuse inflicted on dutiful wives, and finally the poverty they were forced to endure when abandoned by their husbands and other male kin.

White then embarked on the cross-dressing narrative, drawing on a long-standing Anglo-American tradition, although one declining in popularity by this period. The standard plot of most of these accounts tells the tale of a young woman, who disguises herself as a man in order to follow her husband or lover who has gone off to war or to sea. After a series of adventures in war and while on leave, which often include making sexual advances toward other women, the woman and her beloved are eventually united in marriage (Dekker and Van der Pol 1989; Dugaw 1989; Jelinek

1987). Although the cross-dressing narratives seem to threaten and sub-vert gender norms, the threat is a temporary one; in fact the transvestite's re-adoption of female dress and behavior at the end of the story, and its heterosexual resolution reinforce the prevailing gender system. Deborah Samson Gannett's account of her masquerade as a young man and service in the Continental Army during the Revolution, ended with her unmask-ing, and later marriage (Hiltner 1999; Sobel 2000, 191–96; Young 2004). Even Lucy Brewer, the fictional heroine of *The Female Marine* (1815–1819), who is seduced, abandoned, and coerced into prostitution before she escapes and joins the Navy during the War of 1812, ends up happily married (Cohen 1997). At the heart of the majority of the tradi-tional accounts of female transvestism (such as the Female Warrior bal-lads) lies the story of a heterosexual romance. The accounts do present a world turned upside down, but this is a temporary inversion or reversal, which will be righted at the end of the tale (Dugaw 1986).

White and Fisher plot a much more radical course, for at the core of their narratives lay the failure of the heterosexual romance. Domestic hap-piness and marital bliss do not lie in store for them; on the contrary, the failure of their marriages is the source of their travails and their gender transgressive exploits. White disingenuously denies that her masquerade was the result of any deliberate intent on her part. Claiming to have become more masculine as time passed, she argues, "Nature had so 'ordered it' and I could not remedy it" (*Narrative*, 46). So she goes along with nature's decree, amuses herself, and gets herself into trouble. When White takes on the persona of a man she often is mistaken for one by women; men on the other hand suspect her not only of being a man dis-guised as a woman but as a British or French spy. White manages to cross and defy the boundaries of both gender and nation, and even when threat-ened with imprisonment refuses to clarify her identity.

Fisher's one-time masquerade as a man has the potential of being far more subversive than any of White's antics; it is not a mere narrative strat-egy intended to pique the readers' flagging interest, but an open display of wifely rebelliousness and disobedience. In defiance of her husband who sold Jane, an enslaved woman who had been with her since childhood, Elizabeth "borrowed" a man's clothing and set out to rescue Jane. Jane was the only person in the *Memoirs* toward whom Fisher expressed any feelings of love. Using a form of emotional projection found in other accounts when free, white, men and women discussed their emotional attachments toward enslaved people, Fisher projected her emotions onto Jane saying:

". . . went in pursuit of the negro girl who loved me beyond expression" (*Memoirs*, 91).[9] Fisher does not don men's clothing in order to follow a man, but in order to save an enslaved woman whom she loves; with this one act she threatens to subvert the boundaries of both gender and race (*Memoirs*, 90–92).

Both women's narratives ended with an account of their imprisonment. White and Fisher wrote and published their accounts after their release from prison, both in order to present their versions of the events that led to their imprisonment and perhaps in an attempt to earn some extra income. Both tapped in to a long-standing literary tradition of criminal narratives. The early criminal narratives, especially the criminal conversion narratives, had both sacred and secular objectives. Written in prison, most often while awaiting execution, the condemned reflected upon their lives of sin, repented, and sometimes at the end of this process of self-scrutiny and self-assessment they also underwent religious conversion. While these tales of a life of scandal and sin followed by repentance did serve a didactic purpose, cautioning and sermonizing to the readers about the wages of sin, they also titillated their readers, providing a glimpse of a depraved or criminal life (Boudreau 1997; Franklin 1989; Williams 1986). By the early nineteenth century however, the didactic message was fading away, and the narratives became a way for readers to participate vicariously in the risks and excitement of urban criminal life (Branson 1996; Cohen 1999).

In the closing pages of her *Memoirs*, Fisher stated that she underwent a religious conversion while in jail, yet the reader is hard-pressed to take Fisher at her word that her "heart is weaned from the cares of this world— every soul has my best wishes for its welfare" (*Memoirs*, 103). The self-abasement and unconditional surrender often found in conversion narratives is missing from Fisher's account (Juster 1991), despite her protestations to the contrary she remained antagonistic, belligerent, and unreconciled to her fate, promising a revised version of her *Memoirs* where she would prove her innocence (and her brother's guilt).

One of the most important stylistic differences between Fisher's and White's texts is the latter's combination of prose and poetry. Critics have argued that the mixture of genres was often perceived as "a threat to endogamous, hegemonic order" (Favret 1994, 160). In the eighteenth century a well-established gendered literary hierarchy was in place; within this hierarchy women were conceded a place in prose writing while the writing of verse was considered a masculine domain. Throughout the century women novelists often included poetry in their prose texts in order to challenge this gendered division of genres and to stake out ideological claims concerning women's social and intellectual status. By the end of the eighteenth century, poetry in women's novels was also viewed as "the particular language and hallmark of sensibility," signaling her worthiness (Paradise 1995, 67).

Thus, the mixture of prose and poetry is but one rhetorical tactic White employed in order to destabilize her identity and in particular her gender identity. By using a tactic utilized by and associated with female novelists White aligns herself with them hinting at her feminine identity, at the same time she emphasizes her masculine qualities. White's more "masculine" intellectual accomplishments and virtues expressed in the text make up for her "real life" feminine "failures" and her nonadherence to conventional notions of female virtue. If, however, as Christopher Castiglia has argued, White's narrative was "embellished if not entirely fabricated" (1996, 110) then this mixture of genres may also be read as a critique or a parody of the novel of sensibility and its conventions. Late-eighteenth-century male and female novelists are known to have satirized learned women and female poets, as well as the practice of incorporating poetry into prose (Paradise 1995).

The sudden appearance of poems within a prose text (and within the epigraphs discussed later) disrupts the flow of the narrative by freezing a particular moment. They also undermine its unity by visually standing out; these highly composed and formal pieces bestow an artificial quality on the text, which distances it from the surrounding narrative. In spite of White's protestations to the contrary, the effect is that the more her prose "insists upon the spontaneous presence of the poetry, the more the poetry metamorphoses into an unnatural apparition" (Favret 1994, 165). Whether White made conscious use of this effect or not, the fluidity of genres in her text reinforces the theme of gender fluidity which is woven throughout it; by calling attention to the arbitrariness of genre she is simultaneously pointing at the malleability of gender.

White also makes extensive use of epigraphs as part of her paratext. The paratext, which includes titles, chapter titles, prefaces, epigrams, notes, appendixes, etc., establishes zones of transition, mediating between the text and the non-text (Allen 2000, 103). It simultaneously frames and constitutes the text for the readers, suggesting to them how the text should and should not be read. The paratext inflects the text; it signals the readers that several levels of language and meaning are to be superimposed and juxtaposed, mainly in order to produce ironic effect. For example, in chapter 7, White recounts her examination before the magistrates on charges of spying, brought on in part because she was mistaken for a man. While White is quite critical of the magistrates and presents them in a ridiculous light in the course of the chapter, her description could be interpreted as factual and she stops short of name-calling. Her epigram, however, leaves no room for mistaking her opinion of them: "They wanted only ears half a foot long to make them just like asses."

Fisher on the other hand made minimal use of the paratext, consciously employing it only on the title page to her autobiography. As noted previously by Stephen Arch, "[T]he inverted V shape of the paragraph summarizing her story visually draws the prospective reader's eye toward her half brother's name in bold capitals" (2001, 151). Lower down on the page she placed the only epigraph to appear in her memoirs, cluing her readers to the central themes of her narrative: "the perfidy of private friendship," "the persecution of relatives," "the frowns of the world," and "domestic calamities." But more importantly she establishes her response to them, by claiming that none of these "can shake the mind that is armed with conscious virtue."

Fisher referred only once to a text outside her own, the Bible (*Memoirs*, 99). This paucity of external literary references may be the result of the text's objective, which is to augment a legal claim. Fisher took meticulous care in noting facts she could safely establish (dates, names, and places) and as a result the *Memoirs* often reads like an expanded form of a pretrial deposition. The aims of White's *Narrative* are more ambiguous, although entertainment is clearly one of them. White's epigraphs were drawn from a range of genres: essays, plays (mainly Shakespearean), Greek and Roman mythology, poems, anonymous proverbs and sayings, biblical verses. As many of the quotations appearing in the epigraphs (and others embedded in the text) originally appeared as integral parts of other literary works, they immediately trigger off a series of intertextual resonances, which the readers bring to or discover in the text. These quotations compound the heteroglossic problem facing modern readers,[10] as many of these resonances are lost because the original texts, within which the quotations originally appeared, are unfamiliar or have been forgotten.

This discussion of style and genre leads us back inevitably to the question of gender, more specifically to the unresolved question of White's gender identity. A comparison of the two texts and the possible sources of their authors' literacy may provide us with a few more clues on the path to unraveling White's enigmatic persona. White did mention attending school as a young child, both in Boston and in Stockbridge. Her allusions to a variety of other works, however, suggest that her acquaintance with literary texts went far beyond the staple fare of colonial dame schools or a standard female schooling at home. Elizabeth Fisher, who was the daughter of a minister and related (albeit by her father's remarriage) to the Jays, one of the most prominent and well-educated families of the new American Republic, did not display such a familiarity; Fisher makes only one brief reference in the course of her *Memoirs* to her short-lived formal education, where she apparently had acquired the skills of reading and writing. The near absence of intertextual references within Fisher's text, and its factual, almost sparse, writing style may well have been the result of its legal function; however, when combined with her tendency to spell words phonetically, Fisher's writing style suggests that her exposure to a variety of literary texts may have been limited, at best.[11] White seems not only blessed with a "prodigious" education and memory, she flaunts them at her readers. Fisher remained emotionally invested in her past and as she retold the story of her life forgotten or repressed emotions resurfaced. White, on the other hand, was able to distance herself from the retelling of her life's story; her assertive, self-assured, playful, and often self-mocking tone, contrasts with Fisher's angry and belligerent tone.

So was the author of White's *Narrative* a man? It is a possibility that cannot be discounted. In the eighteenth century male writers and journalists often employed female pseudonyms in travelogues, memoirs, articles, and letters. Benjamin Franklin, for example, used this convention extensively in the course of his career, usually to express opinions considered slanderous or illegal. Franklin not only used female pennames (usually allegorical ones such as Caelia Shortface, Martha Careful, and Alice Addertongue), he often went on to fabricate an elaborate background for his personae. Silence Dogood, his earliest persona who appeared in the *New England Courant*, was a middle-aged widow, who commented rather acerbically on New England affairs. Dogood claimed she was born on a ship bound for America. Her father drowned during the sea voyage, and her impoverished mother fostered her outside Boston. Later, she was bound to a country minister and received a good education. Eventually she married the minister and had three children by him. While readers may have speculated on the gendered identity of the author of Dogood's letters, if only because of their author's allegorical pseudonym, nothing led them to suspect a later persona, Polly Baker. Newspaper articles, which reprinted her words, claimed that Baker was an unmarried Connecticut woman, who was brought repeatedly before the magistrates on fornication charges; in the course of her trial she defended her moral character and went on to indict the sexual double standard in a speech, which was transcribed and then printed. The articles go on to claim that Baker eventually married one of the magistrates. "The Speech of Miss Polly Baker" first appeared in 1747 in the London *General Advertiser* and was soon reprinted in newspapers in Europe and America; as far as it is known, Polly Baker's "speech" was accepted as a true account of an actual event and only years later was Franklin's authorship revealed (Hall 1990). Thus, White's *Narrative* may well have been the product of an unknown male author; the expression of proto-feminist sentiments and their veracity should not preclude male authorship of the text. However, White, true to her style, simultaneously sprinkles the text with enough hints to support her claims to the title of "authoress."

FILLING IN THE BLANKS

At the end of her *Narrative*, K. White, who had been deceived by her bigamous fiancé, abandoned by her unfaithful husband, and suffered financial hardships, remains a divorced and impoverished woman, who has been recently released from a debtor's prison. Elizabeth Fisher, who has been repeatedly abandoned by various members of her family, finds herself in a similar situation at the close of her *Memoirs*, poor, widowed, and estranged from her children and her family. K. White would have been in her late thirties and Elizabeth Fisher in her late fifties at the time their narratives were published. While I have been unable to trace White's whereabouts after 1809 (just as I have been unable to substantiate any other event in her life), I know that Fisher died in 1845, at the age of eighty-six in Montreal. What happened to these two women in the following years? Did White ever settle with her creditors? Did Fisher ever get the chance to present the legal evidence she claimed to have held? Did she reconcile with her surviving children or her brother for that matter?

No less disturbing is the way their narratives come abruptly to a halt; disturbing, because I too have been socialized in the conventions of the middle-class autobiography, with its "climax-and-resolution/ action-and-interaction model" which "presupposes an active and reactive world." While White's and Fisher's narratives of self conform in part to middle-class female autobiographies by centering their narratives around their "early life with father and afterlife with husbands," they also defy those conventions, by adopting the "*in medias res* ending," associated with working-class autobiographies (Gagnier 1991, 43).

At the end of *The Handmaid's Tale*, Margaret Atwood puts the following words in the mouth of a historian, who is speculating on the unknown fate of the woman who is the topic of his study: "Our document, though in its own way eloquent, is on these subjects mute. We may call Eurydice forth from the world of the dead, but we cannot make her answer; and when we turn to look at her we glimpse her only for a moment, before she slips from our grasp and flees. As all historians know the past is a great darkness and filled with echoes" (Atwood 1985, 394). In many ways these words apply to the narratives of self White and Fisher wrote. How much do you and I, their readers, really know about these women and what motivated them? We know what they have chosen to divulge to us; they could be lying (consciously or unconsciously, to themselves and to us), they could be telling the truth (all of the time or some of the time). They have left large gaps in their stories and many questions remain unanswered, yet perhaps unwittingly these gaps, pauses, and silences reveal a great deal and enable us to discern the timbre of the echoes.

Fisher, for example, lived in a rural area on colonial New York's frontier, yet she never mentions any of the prerevolutionary land riots that disrupted the region. There is no hint of the Revolution in her account, until the British forces are nearly at her doorstep. Her father and husband were loyalists, yet she never discloses their feelings or beliefs regarding the political issues of the day, nor does she explicitly reveal hers for that matter. It is possible that this silence is a reflection of the general political apathy the rural population of New York displayed toward political matters before the Revolution (Kim 1970; 1982). It may also be likely that knowledge or discussion of such matters was thought to be unfitting for a woman, and such traditional views on appropriate female behavior may have been more prevalent in loyalist households. Mary Beth Norton, who studied loyalist claims, argues that, "late eighteenth-century men, at least those who became loyalists, did not systematically discuss matters of family finances with their wives" (Norton 1976, 395). This attitude may well have spilled over to encompass the political attitudes of the day.[12] But Fisher's actions speak volumes; at the end of the Revolutionary War, despite the fact that her husband had returned to the United States (and her father returned to

Scotland), Fisher decided to separate from her husband and she and her children move back and forth from Canada to the United States. She persisted in conducting her financial affairs independently of her husband and insisted on viewing herself as her ultimate source of authority. Fisher's behavior suggests that the rhetoric of the American Revolution may have had a great impact on ordinary women's sense of self, and it was this new sense of self that was winding its way into the fiction of the period.

Both women are silent about their relationship with their children; a silence I found both puzzling and disturbing. K. White stated that she was pregnant when her husband deserted her, yet this is the last time she ever mentions her child in the *Narrative*. We do not even know if she delivered it safely.[13] Fisher mentions early in her *Memoirs* that she gave birth to five children (*Memoirs*, 89), later on she mentions that by 1800 only three were still living (*Memoirs*, 98). She revealed very few details about these children (no names, dates of birth, or anecdotes); in fact only two of the surviving three were mentioned by name. Fisher neglects to name her own mother and her first stepmother, who died in childbirth.

What does this silence suggest about the perception and experience of motherhood in the postrevolutionary era? Fisher at least was well aware of a new emerging affective style of parenting and her failure to achieve it. She projected the blame for this failure onto her children, citing specifically their "unnatural dispositions" toward her (*Memoirs*, 100). Well into adulthood she remained so fixated on her relationship with her father, stepmother, and half-brother, that all other emotional relationships are subsumed to it. Regenia Gagnier finds that evidence of this kind of abusive, or at best emotionally barren, mother-child relationship can be found in working-class autobiographies well into the twentieth century (Gagnier 1991). Fisher's relationship with her children may or may not be typical, but it does suggest that we need to move well beyond the middle class in our examinations of family relationships, prescriptive notions of motherhood, and the lived experiences of women, and rethink some of the paradigms used in the study of gender in the early republic (see Young [1981] 1993, 286–88).

Historians have argued that the American Revolution was both profoundly radical and deeply conservative (Kerber 1989; Young 1993). The Revolution's radical and conservative gender boundaries have long been illustrated by Abigail Adams's famous "Remember the Ladies" letter, and her husband's tart and worried response regarding a numerous and powerful discontented "tribe." But the extent of the revolutionary ideologies' impact on the daily lives of ordinary men and women, especially their intimate relationships, has often eluded historians. Given the fact the "Republican mother and wife" was supposed to wield (or in the conservative view, contain) her moral authority within the family, it is hardly surprising that marriage and the family became the subject of women's attentions. Al Young states that during the postwar period, "what Abigail Adams had taken up from 1776 on only in the privacy of her letters to her husband was now a matter of public discourse" (1993, 217). In newspaper articles, essays, and plays women debated subjects such as female education, marriage, and the tyranny of husbands (Kritzer 1996); Judith Sargent Murray's essay *"On the Equality of the Sexes"* of 1790 was but one of the more notable of such essays.

K. White and Elizabeth Fisher shared in this political and gendered legacy of the American Revolution, as did the playwrights, novelists, and pamphlet writers who followed them, and in this sense all were daughters of the American Revolution. But this legacy had two faces: a public one, benevolent and affirming, and another, hidden one, repressive and restrictive. While most women, in keeping with the prevailing gender ideology of the time selectively celebrated its public and affirming aspects, others, such as White and Fisher, charted its hidden and repressive ones. Rereading White's and Fisher's narratives (and others like them) reveals that the "hidden transcript," which launched a political critique of the institution of marriage and the position of women within it, was barely concealed beneath a thin veneer of acceptable language, and was probably accessible to its early-nineteenth-century readers. Their refusal to accede wholeheartedly to the "public transcript" marked them as the other, unruly and defiant, daughters of the Revolution.

NOTES

1. The phrase is taken from the title of Linda Gordon's study of domestic violence in Boston (1988).

2. Researchers have usually dealt with White and Fisher in tandem and taken White's gender identity at face value (Arch 2001; Sobel 2000).

3. The precise terms Nussbaum uses are "counteridentify" and "disidentify."

4. An exception to this is Isabelle Lehuu's (2000) excellent study of popular print media in the antebellum period, which examines newspapers, magazines, penny papers, and other publications. One may compare this lively and thriving market to that of the colonial period, as described by David Hall (1996).

5. This political critique of marriage when it appeared, in newspapers for example, was often presented in the form of satire, or ironic verse.

6. Researchers now view animal abuse as part of a constellation of dysfunctional family patterns, establishing a clear link between parent-child violence and animal cruelty. They also suggest that displays of animal cruelty may tend to inhibit the development of empathy in children (Arkow 1996; Flynn 1999).

7. I have chosen to view White as a cross-dresser, rather than a transvestite, mainly because I see her as one following a particular literary tradition focusing on masquerading heroines. This does not mean that White did not derive a great emotional gratification from this activity; gratification, which in current usage, would lead to her definition as a transvestite.

8. Interestingly enough, while White was subscribing to an elite form of honor—the duel—her opponent called her out to a fistfight (see Gorn 1985).

9. Benjamin Rush made a similar comment about William Gruber, an enslaved man he held in bondage for many years (Sobel 2000, 85). Even more telling is the fact that Fisher referred to Jane by her name; in contrast, only two of her five children are ever referred to by name.

10. Heteroglossia is a term coined by the Russian literary theorist, Mikhail Bakhtin (1895–1975). Bakhtin argued that every text is imbued with a multitude of (often contradictory) social and cultural voices. These voices become a major problem, especially when a reader from one place or time reads the text of a writer from another place or time. Much of the multivocality and the nuances of the text are lost as the reader is attuned to and notices only the sounds and meanings with which she or he is familiar.

11. My examination of Abigail Abbot Bailey's *Memoirs* and Eliza Ann Alby's *Life, Adventures* resulted in similar findings.

12. This attitude stands in marked contrast to the behavior of patriot women. Comparative studies from South Carolina (another colony deeply divided between patriots and loyalists) suggest that patriot women in rural areas were far more conversant with their families' economic circumstances, and anecdotal evidence from memoirs, diaries, and letters suggests that in many cases their husbands did consult them on political decisions (Halevi 1995).

13. At the beginning of the chapter (in the highlights) she does state that the baby died in childbirth but does not refer to either her delivery or the baby's death in the course of the chapter.

NARRATIVE

of the

LIFE, OCCURRENCES, VICISSITUDES

and

PRESENT SITUATION

of

K. WHITE

Compiled and collated by herself . . . Feb. 1809.

SCHENECTADY

Printed for the Authoress

1809

PREFACE

IN GIVING THE characters of the times, it ought not to be with a design to inflame the mind or corrupt the heart, but with a laudable desire and intention to contrast vice with virtue, that the former might be hated by being seen, and the latter caressed and admired, as leading to present and future happiness.

Modern living characters will make a stronger impression no [on] the mind, than raking up the virtuous actions of the deceased ancients.

The errors of our own country women will check the vicious career of their sisters, and teach, from their misfortunes, how the pit of misery may be shunned. Perhaps few women have a better claim, to be distinguished for the vicissitudes of life than the authoress; especially in taking a retrospective view of my infant state. Educated from precept and example, by my parents, in the principles of virtue and religion; who never set before my eyes an example of vice, nor ever omitted an opportunity to instill into my mind the principles of virtue.

I am aware of the critics; they have no claim to this production. It is the deliberate and reflecting philanthropic mind, for whom it is designed, and such I am convinced, will throw a veil over any imperfections that may present, and meet with a liberal construction.

Under these impressions I have ventured to usher the following sheets to the public.

The Authoress

∽∾∽

CHAPTER I

The Authoress introduced to the public . . . Her Parentage and Birth . . . Her arrival in America . . . Anecdotes of the Voyage.

. . . . Beware of yonder dog,
Look when he fawns, he bites and when he bites
His venom tooth will rankle to the death.[1]

SHAKESPEARE, RICH. III

CUSTOM has sanctioned the appearance of authors before the public in *propria persona*. Before the awful bar of criticism they are arraigned, and their fate depends on the verdict about to be pronounced. A timid female, unused to so severe and arduous a task, with trembling step, approaches the threshold of her "tale of woe" . . . a "plain unvarnished" tale she is about to unfold. She may indeed be subject to all the weaknesses of her sex, and may therefore have some claim on your pity and indulgence. From these weaknesses she can plead and offer no exemption; her only study shall be to relate *"facts"*. . . . Facts that may emphatically entitle her to a place among the sons and "daughters of woe."

I was born in Edinburgh, the metropolis of Scotland, in the year 1772, and came to America in the year 1775, together with my parents. We set sail in the ship Charming Susan bound for Boston,[2] and laden with merchandize. My father, whose mind was already afflicted with misfortunes, was a merchant, and whose endeavors to gain a fortune had been repeatedly frustrated by the accidents incident to trade, in the loss of ship at sea and other losses. He at length turned his attention to a settlement in the western world, vainly trusting that it would be freed from the persecutions of his evil genius,[3] he engaged a passage for himself, my two brothers and four sisters, with captain L ___, who commanded the ship Charming Susan. Our passage for many days, was uninterrupted by any incident worthy of notice; the captain appeared anxious of making himself agreeable, and the company we had contributed much to the pleasures of the voyage; it consisted of seven male, and seven female passengers . . . one of them in particularly (a Mrs. Carmichael, an Irish lady who had recently lost her husband) was possessed of every accomplishment which could endear her to society; a soft melancholy had stamped its traces on her countenance and added to the interest she was calculated to excite. Captain L ___, (whose real character was that of a professed libertine, and devoid of feeling and humanity) paid her, during the passage, many marked attentions, which were returned by Mrs. Carmichael with a distant coldness and respect; her heart "was not attuned to love," and the captain's manners were far from being pleasing to a female. Few of the passengers, however, except my father, appeared to notice his behaviour, but an occurrence soon attracted the attention of the company. Mrs. Carmichael had one evening received an insulting offer from the captain, couched in still grosser language, and which she had repulsed with disdain; she complained of it to my father and stated that her situation was extremely irksome and that, unless she was relieved from the captain's importunities, she must leave the ship at the first opportunity that offered. My father, whose humanity was sensibly affected by this statement, took the opportunity of remonstrating with the captain. An altercation ensued which terminated in a resolution of all the passengers, to resent the first insult the captain would dare to offer to the lady. A calm ensued and apologies were made and accepted. . . . But, oh! How deceitful this calm . . . a few nights after, the passengers were aroused from their slumber by the cry of "murder, Murder," they rushed to the place from whence it issued and beheld Mrs. Carmichael lying in an agony of distress, and the captain that moment leaving her; no doubt could be entertained of the objects of the captain's visit and of his dastardly attempt upon her honor, which attempt but too fatally succeeded. Without hesitation the captain was put under arrest and continued a prisoner the greater part of the voyage. It may be readily conceived that the time subsequently to this transaction, was not the most pleasant. The mate, who commanded the vessel, was odious to the sailors; he established new regulations and entrenched upon their diet; the sailors, also, reposed no confidence in his natural abilities, but were well assured of the captain's superiority to him in every respect. They demanded his release, and threatened to mutiny in case of refusal; the passengers resolved not to release the captain. No doubt serious contest would have followed, had not a storm set in which required all hands to manage the vessel; and in addition to this, a leak was discovered which kept the pumps constantly at work; the storm continued ten days, during which time it became necessary to lighten the vessel, nay, even to throw overboard some of the water casks. The mate had lost the reckoning and none could ascertain the latitude we were in. What added to our misfortunes was, our being put upon our allowance of water, and our miseries would have been terminated in a very few days by a complete want of it, had not Providence kindly provided against it. A vessel hove in sight! All was joy and confusion; in a few hours we hailed her, and received a fresh supply of water; but what was also equally important to us, we were informed of the ship's bearing and course. Thus relieved, the passengers consented to the captain's discharge upon his parole of honor, not to molest any of the ladies and to conduct himself with perfect propriety. This being adjusted, we arrived in Boston in thirteen days after. Our arrival was, to the passengers, a most joyful event, as for the captain, he was soon arrested by an officer of police and conducted to prison upon the charge of Mrs. Carmichael for the outrage he had committed upon her, during the passage.*

∞•∞

CHAPTER II

Authoress' Education . . . Removal to Stockbridge . . . Taken prisoner by the Indians . . . Her treatment while among them . . . Some account of their Manners and Customs . . . Their Barbarity towards an English prisoner.

> "Misfortune marked thee for her own,
>   And frost-like nipped the very bud of hope."
>
>   ANON.

ALTHOUGH my parents were not the most splendid favorites of fortune, yet that capricious goddess had been bountiful enough to them in the

---

*The principal facts in this chapter were given me by my father, who, also, told me, that the captain was tried and convicted, but had the good fortune to escape from prison and absconded to the East-Indies, that after remaining there some years he was accidentally drowned.

competencies and even conveniencies [conveniences] of life. My prospects were above mediocrity. I was beloved of my parents and the "cold blast of woe" had as yet not ruffled the complacency of my situation. On my father's arrival in America he placed me at school. This indulgent parent knew and appreciated the value of education and the necessity of imparting to the infant mind, the rudiments of virtue and knowledge upon which all our future hopes of happiness must depend. I soon became a favorite at school. The kindness of my tutor flattered me with the opinion that I possessed a mind superior to most of his scholars. I became (tho' a mere girl) fond of my task and would lament the time of my absence from school, as much as some of the scholars would detest their confinement. I was continually loaded with presents for my industry and attention, and by the time I was eight years of age, I was an adept in almost every kind of needle work and embroidery. The war in America now beginning to rage with great violence, I removed from Boston to Stockbridge.[4] About this period too, I must lament the departure of the best of parents for England. His early and deep rooted prejudices in favor of the royal cause, could not be eradicated; his residence in America, therefore became unsafe. The name of "tory" carried with it destruction; disgusted and disappointed he embarked for his native country.

At Stockbridge I was again put to school with a teacher who united in himself every qualification necessary for the instruction of female children. The school was situated in a lonely, unfrequented place, at a considerable distance from any other house, and surrounded in every direction with woods. Here my time was agreeably divided between recreation and study. My schoolmates and myself in leisure hours would frequently stray amongst the woods and engage themselves in picking wild berries, and would sometimes return late to the house. One evening (and an evening I shall always remember with horror) on my return homeward to the school house my companions having gone some distance before me, I was suddenly alarmed with the horrid yells of savages. Conceive the horror of a helpless orphan, a mere child, whose imagination was alive to the tomahawk and the knife, and the yells every moment approaching nearer, my little feet bruised and fretted by the severities and fatigue of running, refused their office. I sat down under a tree almost breathless with agony and despair. I trusted I would remain unperceived. I listened to every breeze which passed, even the rustling of a leaf affrighted me; another yell announced their being nearer! Another, and another succeeded!—I still retained my senses so far as to endeavor to hide myself behind a tree; I rose for the purpose and horrid to relate, that moment I was stuck prostate to the earth by a savage. Immediately he seized me by the hair, and by a whoop, to be equaled only by a demon of hell, he soon collected six more savages at the place where I lay. I gave myself up for lost . . . . they immediately stripped me and tied my hands behind my back; in this situation they forced me to walk the whole night; if I stopped thro' fatigue, I was knocked down and the least delay in rising again was rewarded by kicks and bruises. It will be vain for me to describe the agonies of that night, suffice to say, at the dawn of morning we halted in a retired part of a wood, where shortly after they threw towards me a piece of dried meat, tasting like pork, though since I learnt it was Bears meat, to satiate my hunger. Here we remained till night when they again ordered me to follow them; to refuse was useless. We marched that whole night and continued the same manner of traveling by night and resting by day, for four days more, at the end of which, we arrived at a small settlement of about six or seven huts . . . The moment our arrival was known, I was surrounded by a number of male and female savages, each trying in their turn to injure my feelings and to wound my person. After suffering every insult and injury my human nature was capable of, my infant years sunk beneath the load, I became insensible and swooned away. How long I remained in this situation I cannot determine, but would to God that my senses had never returned. When I awoke, I discovered myself near a large fire surrounded by a circle of Indians. I soon learned my unhappy destiny. Two other prisoners who had been brought to our encampment (if such it may be called) were placed near me tied like lambs for the slaughter. The Indians presented us three small pieces of reed of different sizes and by signs directed us to draw each one of them; they were drawn, and a young man of the name of George Robison became the victim of their hellish fury. I shall pass over the manner of the tortures he experienced, death soon relieved the poor sufferer from the flames! . . . Our feelings, it will be readily conceived, were torn with anguish and indignation; nor were suspence and apprehension that our fate would soon be the same, the least painful. But fortune had other and more painful afflictions in reserve for me . . . The same evening we perceived the savages in council and by their operations we judged that they were about removing farther into country; from our manner of traveling and the situation we were in, I could form no opinion of the distance we had come, nor how near we were to any white settlement. The reader will therefore hardly expect, and that too from a girl of my, then, tender years, a distinct recollection of all the occurrences that took place, or to detail them in the geographical manner. I was sorely bruised and lacerated; my arms were cut almost to the bone, from the withes I was tied with—my mind occupied only by the dread of torture and the devouring flame, tears almost blinded the powers of vision, and fatigue and abstinence had worn down my frame. A small rag of blanket was all my covering, and a few pieces of dried, smoky meat my food. From this painful situation I was aroused by an Indian, who sternly directed me to rise, and brutally pushed me forward. My fellow prisoner, upon whom of violent fever had seized, owing probably to indisposition before his capture and the cruelties he experienced after, fell almost every step he advanced. The savages soon perceived his situation and humanely relieved him from his anguish by the hatchet. I have often felt astonished that, young as I was, my strength still supported me under all these afflictions! But the ways of Providence of are awful and mysterious! We continued on our march two days more and arrived at another Indian settlement rather larger than the former. Here we tarried, as nearly as I can recollect, about three months; during this time, I was employed as a servant in the hut of an old Indian whose wife, it seems, had taken a fancy to me, and was the means I verily believe, of saving my life. In this family was an Indian also, who had a smattering of the English language, he would frequently interpret to me, the conversations which passed, in a broken, half intelligible manner. I endeavored to obtain from him a correct knowledge of our situation; he informed me that his people were king George's people and were fighting the rebels; that all the prisoners they took were destroyed except those that were "purchased back" by their friends, or saved by the old squaws, that the "red-coats" (meaning the British) had tried to save the lives of the prisoners they took, but that his nation would not consent . . . yet, that as I was a "pretty girl" I should not be hurt, but should be returned to my friends if possible; that I should tell no one what he had informed me, and that I should by no means try to escape, for if I did, I would be killed. It was indeed, to this kind Indian I afterwards owed my liberty and return to my friends. During my stay among the Indians I could not but observe the following favorable traits in the character.

1. They were humane to their friends, and generous to excess.
2. Their children were in every respect wholly obedient to their parents.
3. They were punctual in their engagements and never forfeited their word.
4. Whenever a stranger entered the habitations his person was sacred.

I could not discover whether they possessed any certain idea of a future state; they did not openly adore any divinity except, if such may be called their whoopings and dancings at the appearance of a new Moon. The reader, however may form, perhaps a better opinion of their sentiments of a deity and a future state by the following short dialogue which I will recollect, as it was many years afterwards repeated to me by an Indian who was present.

1st Indian . . . Yorontisky* told me this morning he had an ugly dream last night, he says he was in a large field and saw a *white man*, a rebel, drink out of a *red man's skull.*

2nd Indian . . . It cannot mean harm, for the *Great Spirit* would never permit it, and if he did the *red man* to whom the skull belonged, *would rise from his grave*, and hurl it out of his hands.

1st Indian . . . But the *red man* who owned the *skull, sleeps* in his *grave*.

2nd Indian . . . No, not so; he is with the *Great Spirit* where he enjoys himself in *hunting* and *drinking*, etc. etc.

~∞~

CHAPTER III

The Authoress released from captivity . . . Returns to Boston . . . Is addressed by a young gentleman, to whom she becomes engaged be married . . . The tragical [tragic] termination of the courtship.

From opening skies, may streaming glories shine
And saints embrace thee with a love like mine.

POPE'S ELOISA[5]

NOTWITHSTANDING the friendship and attention of my Indian master, I every day became more anxious to return to my friends. I communicated my wish to my interpreter, who bade me "be silent and wait till hunting season was over." How slow the moments were to this period arrived, everyone may conceive. Happily, however, my spirits did not abandon me: hunting season at length was over and my Indian friend needed not to be reminded of his promise. One night after I was retired

---

*A brother of this Indian.

to rest, I felt some person draw me by the hand, half awaked by the intrusion, I changed my position, but the drawing was repeated. I looked around and being moonlight, I discovered thro [through] the cranneis [crannies] of the hut where I laid, an Indian standing near me. I rose in some trepidation; he bade me "make no noise," his voice was familiar to me, and I at length found it was my Indian friend. He bade me take my blanket round me and follow him. I did not want a second invitation but followed him out of the hut. When I came to the door he gave me a small piece of dried meat, and requested me to confide in him as he was about to take me to "my friends." If an angel had announced these tidings to me they could not have been more grateful. I flew rather than walked and about four days I discovered I was near a white man's house! I scarce felt any fatigue tho' [though] I must have suffered very much on the journey. This friendly Indian told me to go to the house as speedily as possible and that he now must leave me; he turned on his heel and I saw him no more; his kindness I shall never forget. In a few moments I reached the house and after some difficulty was admitted. Here I met with kind treatment, was clothed, and in a few days after, as I was sufficiently recruited in my health, was sent in a waggon [wagon] to Boston, to the great joy of my afflicted mother and friends. Shortly after I arrived in Boston my father returned from England and was welcomed by my mother with the sincerest expression of happiness and mutual congratulation. With these kind parents I remained till I was seventeen—an eventful epoch in the history of most females! Till this age of life nothing worthy of particular notice had occurred to me, except what I have already detailed. As is usual with most girls, I received and went into company; endeavored to display all the attractions I possessed, and often imagined them successfully employed. And, alas! on one occasion too successfully indeed! A young American officer by the name of H****C****** soon became acquainted with me. A mutual flame was a consequence of this acquaintance. He was indeed well calculated to make the impression; with an agreeable address and an elegant person, he united most fascinating manners and persuasive eloquence. He was assiduous in cultivating and increasing my regard for him, and soon proposed to me . . . his heart and hand! Young and giddy, as I was, I little knew the too fatal consequences of this attachment. He vowed, and sighed—and I, alas, consented to become his wife. The day was appointed to consummate the hymeneal rites and unite to me to him for—life![6] But fortune had not done persecuting me. The pleasing prospect of happiness was embittered with wormwood and gall![7] H****C****** was already *the husband of another!!* Three years before he became acquainted with me he had been married to a lady in Pennsylvania, whom he had been compelled to abandon by reason of her ill conduct and infidelity! But these facts he had cantiously [cautiously] concealed for me. He had been esteemed a young unmarried man in Boston, and an officer of distinguished integrity and ability. I have at times discovered him in an absence of mind which to me was unaccountable, and for which I often chided him severely. One morning, and about ten days before the day fixed for our marriage, he informed me of the necessity of his immediately going to Philadelphia on urgent business; but promised to return in two or three weeks at most. We parted in tears. In about a fortnight after his departure I received from him the following letter:

Philadelphia, _____

My *dearest K*____

My abrupt departure from Boston you will no doubt pardon on the reflection that indispensable business alone could detain me from you who possess my undivided affection. Yes, my love, I adore you with the most ardent passion. The mutual vows which we have given and received are endelibly [indelibly] engraven [engraved] on my heart, and shall descend with me to the tomb. Since my departure I have been gloomy and dejected. No attempt to divert my attention has been successful. Your image is continually before me. The lock of hair you have presented me is my constant companion, and my only solace under the affliction of an absence rendered doubly severe by the necessity I am under of continuing it for fortnight, or three weeks longer, at the end of which time I shall fly into your arms, and make your mine forever. Remember me to your kind parents and relatives, and believe me to be,

Eternally your's
H ____ C____

Such implicit confidence did I place in the sincerity of my lover that I never entertained a doubt of the facts contained in his letter; but little did I then know that his journey to Philadelphia was to quiet the claims of an abandoned wife who had instituted a prosecution against him for her support! My answer to him was in these words:

Boston, _____

My *dearest* H____

Your letter filled me with the deepest grief to learn that your absence was protracted beyond the time you contemplated when you left Boston. But I must submit to the necessity which separates me from my love, and live only in the hope of seeing you at the time mentioned in your letter. It will be unnecessary to add how sensibly your absence affects me, or how much I am, yours,

K____ W____

This answer was written with a palpitating heart and with trembling hands dispatched to the post office. The three weeks mentioned in his letter expired and yet no H____ came; I became impatient and dejected and sometimes I fancied him treacherous and false and again would dismiss the idea on the recollection of his past assurances and conduct. At length, however, he arrives. I flew into his arms and fainted. In a moment all was forgotten except his tenderness and affection. A second day for our marriage was appointed, and in one week I was to be his for ever! I shall leave to lovers to judge whether the interval between the day of "sacred engagement" and the "bridal day" justifies the antients [ancients] in representing time as possessed of '*wings.*' To me was more like heavy Morpheus than flying Mercury.[8] The week however soon rolled on till the date previous to the appointed time. My lover then informed me he must go a few miles from Boston to see a friend and return that evening . . . The evening arrived and H____ did not appear. To be brief on the subject, the recollection of which to this moment draws tears from my eyes, H____ had taken *arsenic* that evening and was a CORPSE!

The event was soon, too soon, communicated to me; its effects had nearly terminated my miserable existence. Judge my feelings, when on the summit of happiness to be thus hurled into the very depth of complicated woe. For a week I was confined to my room and during two days of that time wholly deprived of my senses. The world, after this, appeared to me a dreary waste on which not a solitary ray of hope could be found; my friends were lost in conjecturing the cause of the sudden and melancholy event of my dear H____ His papers were examined and the cause discovered, amongst the number was a letter superinscribed to "Miss K____ W____." It is as follows:

My lovely and adorable K____

Ere this reaches you the hand that writes it, that hand which was pledged to you, will cease to move . . . desperation appears to surround me on every side. I never can be happy with or without you; forgive the deception I practised [practiced] upon you; *my heart* was yours, tho [though] *my person* was anothers [another's] . . . Wretch that I was, how could I thus cruelly deceived you, but my life shall pay the forfeit of my folly.

It will be expected, and you have a right to demand the cause of this last and fatal act of mine, though my brain is heated to distraction I shall attempt briefly to state the causes which have determined me on it. About three years ago I was married to a daughter of Mr. G____ P____ of Philadelphia; this marriage was the result rather of my father's wishes than of my own choice. I was too young in fact to form a judgment of my own, or to have felt the soft influences of love. About nine months after our marriage I began to suspect an improper intimacy between my wife and Mr. J____ B____ and within a short time was convinced that my suspicions were too well founded. I abandoned her in a few months after and procured an appointment in the army; after being placed in various situations I arrived in Boston when your charms completely subdued me; this induced me to attempt to obtain a divorce from my wife in which I failed for want of proof of her infidelity. She continued to harrass [harass] and persecute me. Hearing I was in this place about to be married, she set off to frustrate my wishes. She arrived here *yesterday*! Curse on my fate—The dye [die] is cast—There is no alternative—On either side exposure and misery are certain. But that shall be mine alone! Adieu. We shall, I hope, meet in a better place.

Adieu, Adieu, Adieu,
H____ C____

∽∞∾

CHAPTER IV

Authoress addressed by S____ W____ who arrives from England . . . Is prevailed upon to marry him . . . Birth of a child . . . Its death . . . S____ W____ deserts his wife . . . Its cause.

Misfortunes never come alone,
But in battalions.

SHAKESPEARE[9]

A MELANCHOLY, which had nearly proved fatal to me, succeeded the tragic death of my lover; my parents permitted me to wear mourning as soon as my health would admit my appearance abroad. About three months after my lover's death, S——— W——— came to Boston, and being distantly related to my father, made his abode with us. He possessed insinuating manners, and by his attention to the family, soon ingratiated himself in my father's esteem. He professed also to pay me a particular regard, and in due time declared himself to my father as my admirer. I could not, however, find a place in my bosom for a second flame, the first having been too ardent to be easily extinguished. It will not be necessary to dwell on all the particulars of this second courtship. My father was strenuous to win my consent to a union with S——— W———. I yielded to his importunity, and our marriage was celebrated in about thirteen months after my lover's death. I cannot say I was altogether indifferent to S——— W———, his apparent sincerity and attentions had nearly closed the wound which the death of my lover had occasioned; and for several months I had no reason to lament by having bestowed my hand on him. But he was practically a hypocrite; he had no sense of honor, but his depravity was concealed under a veil which in time was removed only to display the consummate powers of treachery and falsehood. Forgetful of his former assiduities, he had the baseness to form an intrigue with my chambermaid . . . robbed her of her innocence and then inhumanely left her a prey to her own conscience and a burden to the community. The fruits of this amour was an infant who with its mother was abandoned by him to the scoffs and insults of an unfeeling world. To aggravate his cruelties, he fled from Boston and deserted me, then far advanced in a state of pregnancy. Thus I was deprived of a lover by suicide and of a husband by his own villainy and depravity.

∽◦∽

CHAPTER V

Authoress enters into trade . . . Her embarrassments occasioned by her husband's creditors . . . Fails in trade . . . Is charged with forgery and acquitted . . . Leaves Boston . . . settles in Providence (R. Island) and engages again in trade.

SUBSEQUENT to my husband's departure, I remained with my brother in law [brother-in-law] in Boston. The state of my mind was wretched beyond description. I was borne down under pressure of calamities all tending to convince me that:

> "Happiness below,
> Is but a fleeting flower that fades as soon
> As the rude hand of misery and woe
> Shall grasp it, ..."

The idea of remaining a burden to my friends was extremely painful; my husband, in his precipitate flight, either from want of time to remove it, or from a more honorable sentiment of compassion towards his wife and offspring, had left me a property worth perhaps about two thousand dollars. The confidence I entertained of my own talents led me to believe that by entering into business as a merchant, I might acquire an independency, or at least, a competancy [competency].[10] I made the attempt; I commenced business as a merchant with a small assortment of goods, and for some time to great advantage; fortune *seemed* (and only *seemed*) to have forgotten for a while her cruel persecutions; and for the sportive goddess soon recalled to mind that I "was still her victim."[11]

My husband's creditors (who were numerous) began to be clamorous for payment of their demands; they saw his wife with a handsome property belonging to him trading in the very town in which they resided; the temptation to wrest this from my possession was too sweet to be resisted . . . Process was entered against me by them and I was summoned to answer in court. Alarmed at this procedure, I resorted to counsel who recommended to me to adjust with the creditors without delay. The consequence was I assumed the debts which my husband owed and continued my trade. At the end of eighteen months I discovered myself worth considerable *less than nothing*; my abilities for merchandize been less than I expected, I had been made the dupe of too many of my customers, and bankruptcy stared me in the face. I was in arrear at least three thousand dollars, and goals and sheriffs became the constant theme of my meditations. Another occurrence also alarmed my mind and jeopardized my liberty. I was charged with *forgery*! The circumstances leading to this charge I shall briefly mention. After my husband's departure I examined the papers he left with me and amongst the rest I discovered a note of hand for about fifty pounds signed by one L_____ P_____, which with some other obligations I caused to be put in suit, L_____ P_____ appeared and contended that the note was *altered* in the date of it and in the *sum* to be paid. The consequence was he applied for warrant against me and I was arrested. Fortunately I found good security for my appearance at court and was set at liberty. I accordingly appeared, was arraigned and tried for this pretended forgery before a court of sessions in the county of Worcester . . . unacquainted with the forms of law, I employed counsel who on the day of trial managed the cause for me. The court was unusually crowded by an audience attracted with the novelty of the scene and various opinions were entertained as to the fate of my defence. I challenged a number of the jury who I knew had prejudices against me, till at length a full jury were sworn; the trial continued to late in the evening when after a very honorable and impartial charge from the court the jury retired and in ten minutes time returned a verdict of *not guilty*. As L____ P____ was very odious in society, and as I was generally believed to be innocent, a shout of applause was given by the audience immediately on hearing the verdict which with some difficulty was silenced by the court. I was now discharged from court and did not discover that I had suffered much with the public in point of reputation. The charge of perjury was justly viewed as a malicious fabrication set on foot by some of my foes with a design to persecute and destroy me.

My pecuniary circumstances were as yet not suspected to be deranged but I soon found that concealment for much longer time was vain. Having received letters from Providence, in Rhode Island, representing that I might, do well in that place, and having some relations there, I form the resolution of removing to that town. I accordingly set off for Providence and on my arrival engaged a store and entered into business there. Here again I was followed by my husband's creditors and threatened with prosecutions; accounts were daily presented against me and every moment I expected to be incarcerated in a dungeon. Driven and persecuted from place to place, I almost despaired of ever being in a state of quietude and peace. I knew that to remain longer in Providence would be dangerous and I therefore resolved to leave it as soon as possible.

◈

CHAPTER VI

The authoress leaves Providence in consequence of her embarrassments . . . Goes to the state of New-York . . . Visits many places in that state . . . Suspected at Schenectady to be a man in disguise . . . While so suspected receives advances from a young lady and engages to marry her! . . . The whimsical denouement of this courtship . . . She leaves Schenectady.

> "Yes truly I was taken for a
> MAN tho' indeed I looked very well
> AS WOMAN considering I weighed 14 stone
> good weight
> But I will be revenged of them for the
> affront. . . .

SHAKESPEARE[12]

ALL my attempts to acquire a competency having proved abortive; driven from place to place, life had lost all its attractions. I had scarce a solitary

hope of tasting its sweets. With these feelings I arranged my affairs in Providence and left in disgust on the 25th February 1801, and on the 2d March
ensuing, after a fatiguing passage arrived in Lansingburgh, in the county of
Rensalaer and the state of New York. In Lansingburgh I remained but one
night and set off for Schenectady the next morning, and put up at Mr.
Gilbert's tavern, where I remained ten weeks. A public house did not altogether please me altho' [although] I had a room to myself and was introduced to many of the ladies and gentleman in that city. In this part of my
memoirs it will be proper to state a circumstance with which my readers
ought to be acquainted. Although in my younger years I was of slender
form yet as I advanced in age, I became large in stature somewhat of a masculine form, of a robust strong complexion, so that upon the whole I would
not make a bad appearance as a *man*, were I dressed in masculine attire.
My female readers will perhaps smile at the fact, but Nature had "so
ordered it" and I could not remedy it.

While at Mr. Gilbert's I was not disposed to correct an opinion which
prevailed with some who saw me, on account of my figure etc. that I was
a *man in disguise*. The suspicions served to amuse me, and in some measure, to divert my attention. A young lady of agreeable deportment who
was in habits of intimacy at Mr. Gilbert's, being one day on a visit to Mrs.
Gilbert, observed me as I entered my room, struck with my appearance she
enquired, after my leaving the room, who I was. My landlady answered,
that all she knew, was, but I was a lady from one of the eastern states, upon
which the young lady observed, that she suspected me, for my appearance,
to be a *man*; to which opinion my landlady seemed to assent. A few days
after, I received a billet in these words:

THURSDAY

"Miss. E_____ J_____

"Having observed at Mr. Gilbert's the few days since, a certain person in
woman's attire and judging that circumstances had rendered this disguise
necessary to conceal the sex of the party, wishes to have an interview with
the person at Mr. Gilbert's this evening at eight o'clock. Should E_____ J_____
be corrected in this belief, she wishes it understood, that the designed interview, is with the best intentions of relieving distress under whatever form it
may be found . . . If incorrect she wishes this note to be destroyed."

Directed, *"To the unknown person at Mr. Gilbert's."*

I received this billet from Mrs. Gilbert, who mentioned that I was a person thereby intended. I read it to with some surprise intermixed with the desire to have some amusement on the occasion. I immediately penned the following answer which I sent to the lady:

"The unknown person to whom Miss E＿＿ J＿＿ had the goodness to address a note this morning does not feel at liberty to be explicit in answering Miss E＿＿ J＿＿'s polite billet at this time and in this manner. This much however, may be said, the interview will be received with extreme pleasure at the time appointed, when Miss E＿＿ J＿＿ shall be satisfied on the subject of her enquiries."

This answer been dispatched, I prepared myself for the appointment with considerable alacrity; as my *chin* wanted the masculine appearance of a *beard*, I supplied the deficiency in the best manner I could. The hour being arrived, I went to my chamber, directing Mrs. Gilbert to send the lady when she came up to my room. A few moments after the hour she mentioned in her note to me, she entered my room, apparently much embarrassed. I desired her to be seated, when the following dialogue passed between us.

"I presume, Madam, she said you are somewhat surprised at the liberty I have taken in calling here; believe me, it was with good intentions; if however you are really a woman, let me no longer remain in suspense." "I feel so much obliged to you, answered I, for your solicitude for my welfare, but I cannot but to render you my unfeigned thanks for your kindness. I am indeed unfortunate, your goodness however is entitled to an explicit answer. I am, *not what I appear to be* . . . I have been *otherwise than what I appear*," (alluding to my *former* and *present* situation in life. The reader will doubtless censure this equivoque, and justly too. I feel its full weight, I could have wished to have omitted this incident had not a regard to *truth* compelled me to narrate it.) "Then you are a *man*," cried she with some surprize [surprise] mixed with pleasure, "and pray, sir, may a perfect stranger to you be so bold as to enquire the motives of concealing your sex? For without flattery, it may be said that your appearance as a *man* would in many respects conduce to your happiness." "Madam," answered I, "my life is a continued scene of misfortune and distress. I have from my cradle been the child of woe . . . your benevolence towards me is an evidence however of my not being totally deserted by the world; I shall, at your request, relate the important parts of my life." Here I gave her a brief sketch of my parentage, birth etc. consciously avoiding any express declaration of my sex. To conclude this interview, she consented to call it the next evening at Mr. Gilbert's, and we pledged our honor to each other to observe secrecy in relation to what passed between us.

The next evening she called and we had an agreeable tete a tete [tête-à-tête]. Her visits were continued for some time and an *engagement* (do not smile, reader) *of matrimony* was actually made between us; the denouement, however, was not altogether so agreeable. A young gentleman who had observed her frequent visits to Mr. Gilbert's and being passionately fond of her, was determined to be a spy upon our conduct. One evening standing at the door of my room he overheard our conversation and abruptly burst in upon us to the very great astonishment of the lady and myself. After making a severe charge against me of attempting to seduce a lady in a disguise, unmanly and indecorous, he commenced an attack upon me with his cane, which I resisted and fortunately left my room without much injury.

To remain longer in Schenectady was obviously improper, and I left next day with reflections not the most agreeable . . . Indeed for this part of my life, no apology can be offered, and I can only trust, therefore, to the indulgence of my readers to pass by a freak of the moment which my better judgment wholly condemned.

࿋

CHAPTER VII

Authoress removes to Herkimer county . . . Is there apprehended as a French spy . . . Her examination before the magistrates, and is discharged . . . Authoress robbed of a sum of money . . . Is afterwards arrested for debts contracted while in trade, and committed to prison . . . Friendship of the sheriff in prison.

> Robed in justices' seat say you?—Why 'tis mockery.
> They wanted only ears half a foot long to make
> Them just like asses.
>
> —Anon.[13]

HAVING discharged my bill Mr. Gilbert's, I set out in the stage for German-Flatts without even once bidding adieu to my charming Miss E____ J ____, and leaving her and her quondam lover to adjust the difference between them. On my arrival at German-Flatts on the 23d June, I put up at a Doctor Griswold's (a public house,) and having a demand against a Mr. B____ W ____ of that place, in behalf of my father, I sent to him for payment. He called and paid the debt he owed me, and afterwards invited me to spend a few days at his house. This invitation was accepted with pleasure—The state of my finances were such as to render it very agreeable. I accordingly went to his house, but in a few days after was placed in a very disagreeable situation: my masculine appearance again afforded ground of suspicion, and three very sagacious justices had very wisely judged the I was come to spy " the nakedness of the land."[14]— In short as nobody knew who or what I was, they concluded I must necessarily be a *French Spy!* a perfectly logical deduction, indeed! An officer, (a catchpoll) was dispatched to apprehend me. He approached with the following address: "Madam—Zir—I zay, Madam—Zir—I have got von varrant vor you." I could scarce comprehend his meaning till he made it perfectly comprehensible by a violent slap on my shoulder and saying I "vos hees brisoner." I entreated him to inform me for what: "Dat you shall zoon zee—zo, gome along wid me to the justasses." By long persuasion, however, he shewed [showed] me his warrant—This was however very little information to me, for the scroll was perfectly illegible, and no human being but the sagacious justices themselves could have deciphered it. The only thing I perfectly understood, that I must go six miles with my lord the catchpoll to appear before the high and mighty lords, the three justices of Herkimer county. Conscious that I owed obedience to the laws of my country, whether pronounced like the braying of an ass or in the soft notes of the nightingale, I tamely submitted, and told Mr. Catchpoll I was ready to attend him.[15] We accordingly proceeded together in a waggon [wagon] to the place of meeting for the justices to examine me. Having arrived, I found the justices gravely seated in the bar-room of an inn, and like so many atlasses [atlases] supporting the whole universe of nature. I was announced as the prisoner, and pen, ink and paper, were called for to take my examination. After one or two potent draughts of liquor somewhat resembling rum and water, one of the justices desired me to be seated. Having gravely opened his lungs with three hems, he thus commenced his examination—

Justice—And pray Sir, or Madam, what may be your name?

Answer—Can that be interesting to either of you in any possible shape?

Justice—We must know or must commit you—we must also know if you are a man or woman?

Answer—Pray, Sir, look at my dress and judge for yourselves.

Justice—Where were you born?

Answer—I was born at my father's house.

Justice—We want to no impertinence—answer explicitly.

Answer—I was born in the kingdom of Scotland.

Justice—How long have you been in this country?

Answer—That I cannot answer from my own knowledge—I was a child when I came.

Justice—And pray where was your last place of residence?

Answer—About six miles from the place where you honors directed me to be taken into custody.

Justice—And pray what is your business in this part of the world?

Answer—That is my own concern; I keep my own secrets.

Justice—You shall know it is our concern also—We wish your answer.

Answer—I came here for business and pleasure.

Justice—Are you single or married?

Answer—I am married.

Justice—Where is your husband, or if you are a man where is your wife?

Answer—My "husband or wife" is in Canada.

Justice—How you support yourself?

Answer—By good eating and drinking.

Justice—That is no answer—How do you gain your livelihood?

Answer—By hard industry.

Justice—What occupation do you follow?

Answer—Travelling.

Justice—To answer what purpose?

Answer—Pleasure.

The justices perceiving that their examination produced nothing conferred amongst themselves. One was of opinion that I was a vagrant and ought to be removed to Scotland where I came from. Another (an Irish justice,) declared "Upon his shoul (soul) he believed me to be a *French Rap* . . . come here as a spy." And the third, (a wise Dutchman) said, "as for my bart, I dink hur to be one rubber." Not agreeing among themselves they adjourned to another room to consult. There they remained two hours, and from the noise they made I suspected them to devote their attention more to Bacchus' libations then to the decision of the important case before them.—In the interim the constable attempted to gain from me the fact the justices wished. Here however he also failed, and he declared with an oath that I "vos a bad man and a teef." the justices having returned, they declared that I must remain prisoner till morning for farther examination. I complained, but in vain, of this illegal deprivation of my liberty. I was obliged to remain at the tavern till morning, when two of the justices again assembled, (the third having gone home.) I was again examined, and the Irish 'squire undertook the task.

> *Justice*—So, my honey, can you not tell the magistrates what occupation you follow?
>
> *Answer*—I have told them all I intended to say.
>
> *Justice*—Och now, do you not know we can compromit [commit] you to prison for your obstropolousness?
>
> *Answer*—You may, but you shall know the consequences of it.
>
> *Justice*—Och, my dear and now be so good and so obliging as to save us the trouble of axing [asking] any more questions—are you a French spy?
>
> *Answer*—If I am, I can only spy out jackasses in this part of the country—I humbly ask your pardon, I meant justasses.
>
> *Justice*—We want none of your impertinence, honey.
>
> *Answer*—I am equally desirous of having none.

Here my second examination ended, and another day I remained under arrest. On the morning of the third day I was liberated from these blockheads without farther enquiries from them. But I was determined to have satisfaction for the injury. I therefore employed a lawyer who had these great justices arrested for false imprisonment at my suit. The consequence was, the justices made the most humble apologies to me for the conduct towards me, and I dropped the prosecution.

While in this town I lost almost all the money I had with me, it being taken from my trunk in my absence.—This placed me in the very disagreeable dilemma, as my finances were indeed rather slender before this accident.—I shortly after suspected a man in the neighborhood, and on suspicion only caused him to be apprehended for the theft. Having been put under keepers, he sent for me, confessed the fact and restored a small part of the money. He was then set at liberty on my representation, and immediately after disappeared.

I now began seriously to reflect that my wandering situation was equally dreadful with that of being at home surrounded with enraged creditors. I therefore determined on returning to my friends and "brave the storm" in preference to becoming, like the "wandering Jew,"[16] a citizen of the whole world. After several fruitless attempts to leave Herkimer county, I set off in a sleigh for the east homewards on the seventh of February— but alas! my intentions were again defeated. On the second day of my journey I was arrested for debt, and my trunk with all my money and effects therein, (excepting a gold watch I had in my pocket with a small sum of money) were taken from me, and I was committed to Herkimer county gaol. While in confinement other writs were issued against me, and my imprisonment promised to be perpetual!—Without a friend to assist, and scarce a penny to save me from starving . . . stripped of the little property I had and cast into prison. Here I cannot omit to notice the benevolence of the sheriff whose humanity to me deserves my eternal gratitude.— While in prison deeply impressed with my forlorn conditions I penned the following lines:

TO LIBERTY

YES! charming goddess,—though bereft of thee,
    I know thy worth, and thy sad loss deplore;
Shall not these eyes again thy beauties see?
    Must not thy graces be to me—no more?
Without thee, goddess, what is all our toil?
    What all our labors, golden stores and wealth?
Can they be equal to a single smile,
    When thou shall bless us with thy sister Health?

To range the valley—breathe the vernal air,
    Own no proud tyrant's haughty power and will:

Can Peru's wealth with joys like these compare,
    If wealth with slavery be united still?

Poor let me be, yet *Liberty* be mine,
    I shall not envy monarchs on their thrones—
But, ah! In dungeons thus to sigh and pine,
        Where tears succeed to tears and groans to
        groans.

'Tis death—'tis worse—of Liberty bereft,
    The world becomes a melancholy waste—
What of enjoyment or of life is left,
    When doomed the cup of slavery to taste?

Ah! Shall these walls for ever hold my frame?
    Shall they alone bear witness of my grief?
Is there no friend to sooth my bosom's pain?—
    No friend, alas, draws near to give relief.

Let me then die—a wretch forlorn and lost,
    Nor let a stone point out the place I lay—
Though once the pride of parent's and their boast,
    I shall be then fast changing into clay.

⌒◦◦⌒

CHAPTER VIII

While in prison the authoress hears of her husband's having married a lady and settled in Canada . . . Authoress discharged from prison . . . Pursues her husband to Canada . . . Has an interview with him . . . Its result.

> "'Tis false—my husband treacherous! No—my life
> on't he's true."—Thus I dreamed last night, but I
> found it to be . . . only a dream.
>
> DAPHNE TO LAON.[17]

WHILE thus indulging my melancholy reflections on a prison, I was called to a subject which had for some time escaped my immediate attention, namely, my ungrateful husband. By a letter I received through a very circuitous route, and which by mere accident ever came to my hands, I learnt that he had married a lady in one of the southern states, and with her had gone to Canada, where he settled. Though I cannot conceal that this intelligence discomposed me considerably, yet I easily reconciled it with his former base and cruel conduct towards me. The picture of his vices wanted but this one shade to render it a masterpiece of its kind. Thus was I doubly distressed by misfortunes,—a lost husband—and lost liberty!—Griefs thus accumulated would have borne down the fortitude of the greatest heroine; how much must it have preyed upon spirits like mine.—The reader will in this place pardon the introduction of a few lines I wrote on the occasion.

TO MY HUSBAND

AND could you thus your plighted faith despise?
    Could you thus forfeit every vow you made?
Ah, why did you so cruelly disguise,
    To say you *loved* when you but meant *betrayed*?

Was falsehood then congenial to thy soul,
    Was truth too odious to become thy friend?
Was vice too stubborn to admit control?
    Or thy proud heart to virtue's rules to bend?

Blush not! If e'er a blush suffused thy face,
    But answer thus,—"'twas nature formed me
        beast—
I claimed not kindred to the human race,
    Long since this tye, and only tye, has ceased."

The severity of the last verse can only be justified by his base desertion from me, and his subsequent as well as prior detestable conduct.

Four months and two days had already silently rolled on and a prison was still my doom. O Liberty! when shall I again be blessed with thy smiles?—"Soon," whispered my guardian genius;[18] but I deemed the expectation to fallacious to be indulged. To urge on what to me appeared the slow and languid wheels of time, I devoted my attention to reading, and occasionally to composition.—I shall add a few more verses which I composed while in prison.

ON THE WORLD'S CRUELTY.

AH, where shall I wander, I cried,
    The world has no pleasure for me—

In yonder deep cavern I'll hide,
    No mortal again shall I see.

I'll dwell with beasts of the field,
    They'll no be more cruel to me
Than Man in whom baseness concealed—
    —To the forest, oh! then let me flee.

The wolf is a friend to its kind,
    His kindred he will not devour,
But man, who can boast of mind,
    Destroys all he has in his power.

His vows are more idle than straws,
    His honor is scarce worth a song;
To the weak 'tis alone he gives laws,
    Which like cobwebs are broken by the strong.

His delight is in woe and distress,
    He's pleased with all rapine and lust
Though truth he alone will profess,
    Yet place in his honor no trust.

For woe and misfortune betide
    The wretch who believes the fond tale;
The victims he'll stab who confide,
    And his honor—he gives to the gale.

Ah! Where shall I wander? I cried,
    Shall peace no more visit my breast?
Must I down life's current swift glide,
    And still be a stranger to rest.

ON SUICIDE

[Occasioned by reflections on my first lover's death.]

STAY, my fond Henry, stay the poisoned glass,
    Life still has comfort to the wretch to give—
Oh! We may yet our lives in pleasure pass,
    And for my sake, if for none other, live!
'Tis I entreat—'tis mine the voices you hear,—
    That voice you once delighted to obey—
O let my cheeks not know the mournful tear,
    Which must o'erspread them if my love's away.

> Awful the scene eternity will show,
>   If rashly this you dare the horrid deed,
> Cannot those tears which for you only flow,
>   Restrain the hand which makes my blood bleed.

While thus indulging myself in occasional reading and composition, and believing my liberation at a distance, the hand of benevolence was extended to my relief ere my most sanguine expectations could have realized. I was discharged from prison by a *friend*, who, which noble disinterestedness, extricated me from my difficulty. Heaven reward for him for his humanity! His name would do honor to these memoirs, but his delicacy permits it not to be mentioned. With the aid of this generous friend I was enabled to effect the purpose I had contemplated, of going to Canada to see my husband. I accordingly started in the sleigh, and without any material occurrence arrived at Queenstown (only a few miles from the residence of S ____ W ____) on the 2d February, 1804. Having put up at an excellent public house, I sent a message to him, concealing my name and the object of the message, directing the messenger only to inform him that a stranger in that part of the country wanted much to see him, and that no apology would be received. The feelings of my mind at this time I shall leave to my reader to conceive, for I am inadequate to their expression.—The interview with him, tho' much desired by me, was still apprehended with terror. S ____ W ____ at length arrived. I desired my landlord to give me a room, and not to admit to any other person than S ____ W ____. I retired it into the room previous to my husband's arrival and threw myself on a bed. My mind was sorely distressed—of flood of tears came seasonably to my relief. Towards evening S ____ W ____ arrived, and being in the bar-room, adjoining my room, I soon recognized his voice in the enquiries he made of the landlord whether the person who had sent for him was at his house. The landlord directed him to my room.—Since S ____ W ____ had left me I had been considerably altered in my appearance, so I readily concluded to my person would be unknown to him. S ____ W ____ entered my room. 'Twas fortunate I was seated, for I trembled so much that I should certainly have fallen on his entrance. He bowed as he entered, and upon seeing me, enquired whether I was the lady who had sent for him. I answered him in the affirmative. I requested him to take a seat, and being seated I told him I wished a few moments conversation with him. The conversation was nearly as follows:—

Authoress—I send for you, sir, to make a few inquiries relating to a subject of some consequence to you, and infinitely more to me.

S. W.—I shall with pleasure, madam, give you every satisfaction in my power—be pleased to proceed.

Authoress—Were you at any time an inhabitant of Boston previous to your settlement here?

S. W.—I was, madam, many years since.

Authoress—Were you at that time acquainted with the family of the name of W ____ ?

S. W.—Yes, Madam, they are distantly related to me.

Authoress—Did you know of a lady of the name of K ____ W ____ ?

I examined his features with attention when I put this question to him. I perceived he was agitated—his lips quivered and his countenance changed. With some hesitation he answered:

S. W.—I was—Madam—ac-quainted with such a lady—but—it is—many years—since—and I have—but—a faint recollection—of the—person.

Authoress—Traitor!—Villain!—Base wretch!—Is your memory as treacherous as your soul?

S. W.—Madam—madam—may I inquire why these harsh epithets?

Authoress—Dare are you ask?—Dare you look at me and not be struck with a conscious sense of your baseness?—I am K ____ W ____ I was once your wife. Would to God my bridal day had been the day of my death.

What further passionate declamations I made in this paroxism [paroxysm] of grief and indignation I cannot recollect.—S ____ W ____ rose and begged of me to be less clamorous—he would explain.

Authoress—Explain!—Wretch!—What can you explain it but to convince me of your hypocrisy and villainy?

S. W.—I entreat you—madam, to hear me—I shall conceal nothing. I am married in this country, and in present circumstances it would be impossible for me to do you ample justice: so far as I can do it rest assured it shall be done. But you must be conscious to expose me in this country can answer no other purpose than driving me to a state of desperation.

Much conversation of a similar nature ensued which I cannot detail in the manner it took place. It resulted, however, in his assurances that he would make ample provision for my future support, and as earnest of his good intentions presented me with Seventy Dollars and a silver watch. He agreed also to settle an annual stipend upon me, and promised to have the papers arranged and executed in a few days. As I most heartily detested the wretch, I cared not for his person, and was well contented to see him no more provided he performed his promises to me.

I waited in Canada several days to see if S ____ W ____ would fulfill his engagement. For some cause or other S ____ W ____ never came again to see me, upon which I left the business in the hands of an attorney, and prepared to return to the state of New-York.

∽∾∾

CHAPTER IX

Authoress returns to the state of New-York . . . Passes by Buffaloe-Creek to Onondaga county . . . Humorous anecdotes at the Buffaloe-Creek of the jealousy of a gentleman of the authoress' intimacy with his wife . . . Is pursued by the husband, who finding the resolution and firmness of the authoress, is content to abandon the pursuit.

> Say, should a fool's-cap on his head be placed,
> Or should his brows by antlers still be graced?
> He debt so causeless female faith suspects,
> Should not the blockhead find what he expects?
> A brace of horns say you?

GARRICK[19]

HAVING made arrangements to leave Canada, I bade adieu to the dominions of his Britannic majesty, and once more reached the land of liberty and safety. I crossed at fort Erie in a scow on the 9th of February, 1804, and reached Buffaloe-Creek, where I put up at the tavern of a Mr. H ____. It would seem that this Mr. H ____ was not altogether satisfied with the fidelity of my landlady, his wife; and when she returned from conducting me to my chamber for the night, where she had some conversation with me, I overheard a warm altercation between them, in which I could distinctly understand that I was the subject of it; that he was censuring his wife for remaining so long in the chamber alone with a *man in women's clothes!*—Thus was my form again become a subject of suspicion. I however remained there that night, and having taken my breakfast next morning I left it. I could perceive that his eyes were continually fixed upon me during breakfast, so I acted as if I did not notice him. Having travelled [traveled] some miles I heard the noise of horses' feet behind my sleigh, and turning round to see who it was, perceived this jealous husband on full gallop to overtake me. I directed the servant to stop my horses, and the fellow soon came up to me and addressed me in very abusive terms. I told him since he judged me to be a man I would act upon it, and presented him my brace of pistols. On the appearance of the pistols, and finding me resolute, he turned his horse and cowardly returned the way he came! Thus much for a jealous husband.

After this foolish adventure I continued my route to Onondaga and put up at Captain Foster's public house, where I received excellent entertainment.—Intending to say a few days here, I penned the following lines:

TO JEALOUSY

THOU green-eyed monster, ne'er at rest,
    Foe to peace and pleasure;
By hateful demons e'er possest,
    Pains thy greatest treasure.

Ever brooding fancied woe
    In imagination;
Jealousy, thy phantom know
    Is thy own creation.

Through a coloured glass you view
    The actions of another;
Their errors of the darkest hue,
    While *your* own you smother.

Your bosom's like the hottest coal,
    Which you set a burning;

So stupid is your gloomy soul,
    Your peace you're ne'er discerning.

In the grave alone you rest,
    And there you're hardly easy;
The demons that disturbed your breast
    Will there be sure to seize thee.

Ah! hated monster, may my mind
    In thy deceits ne'er riot;
All I ask—and be resigned,
    Is give me peace and quiet.

ON MY MASCULINE APPEARANCE.

'TIS said a Pope to Cath'lic's known,
Called in the calendar 'Pope Joan,'[20]
    Was but a timid female:
With me the scene is quite reversed,
My form with which dame nature cursed,
    Gives quite another tale.

Though petticoats, the clothes I wear,
The unrivalled empire of the fair,
    (If Highlanders excepted)
Yet none believe (how sore 't does vex)
That truly it denotes my sex
    No woman I'm accepted.

'Tis true I'm strong and masculine,
What then? My size is mine,
    If living well can make it;
The fat I boast I've justly gained,
Yet if another it has claimed,
    Why he is free—to take it.
I'm sure I'll not refuse the gift,
Nay, gladly give the one a lift,
    Who wished to take it from me:
But vain the attempt the maidens cry,
And the men are even grown so shy,
    That my *fond* husband flees me.

So I must drag the weary load,
Along the life's craggy, up-hill road,
    Nor cannot shake it off;
So e'en content faith I'll remain,
No jeers shall give my bosom pain,
    Nor any fopling's scoff.

∼∾∽

CHAPTER X

Authoress meets with an insult, and challenges the offender to fight a duel . . .
Challenge accepted, and afterwards the affair settled by apologies from the
party challenged . . . Authoress arrives in Albany.

"*L. Bol.*—Did she fight, say you?

Servant—Aye, my Lord, and made his cowardly
soul shudder within him.—She possesses true
genuine courage, and wants but a *breeches* to make her a man.

DIAL. BETWEEN L. BOL. AND SERV.[21]

DURING my stay at Captain Foster's one incident only took a serious turn
and promised to terminate very disagreeably. Aside from that my time was
very agreeably occupied. A gentleman of the name of F____ had circu-
lated a report highly injurious to my reputation and implicating me in a
detestable plan, no less than that of having correspondence with the
British government in Canada, to invade this country. I pretended for
some days not to notice it, as being unworthy of belief; but finding it to
gain upon the public opinion, and causing many people to shun my
acquaintance, I was at length compelled to notice it. I accordingly wrote
a note to Mr. F____ of the following purport:

TO Mr. F____

SIR,

Independent of the claims a *woman* may have upon the liberality and
candor of the other sex, your conduct in vilifying my reputation can admit of
no apology. I am conscious of ever having committed a single act to warrant
the construction you have given to my residence here, or to the foul tales you

have so assiduously attempted to circulate in relation to me. You must be aware of the delicacy of my situation in this part of the country. Without a protector to avenge my wrongs and justify my innocence, you have dared to traduce my reputation and to wound my feelings, trusting the fallacious hope that a woman's weapons were but her innocence and good conduct. But Sir, you shall find I am not totally destitute of others. Your vanity—your courage (if you possess any) shall be put to the test. I have feelings which will not be insulted with impunity, and a resolution to punish the daring assassin of my reputation. It will be in vain for you to decline the call and give you in this note. You shall not resort to the flimsy pretense of my being a woman to excuse your acceptance of it. I am content to waive the distinction with which society has marked the walks in life of the two sexes, and demand therefore that you meet me to-morrow morning, at six o'clock, about a quarter of a mile behind the house of Mr. Foster, in a retired part of the wood, to give me satisfaction. My life or your's [yours] shall "pay the forfeit" of the interview. Weapons should be provided for the purpose.—I await your answer by the bearer.

I am, Sir,
Your obedient serv't
K____ W____

In about an hour I received the following answer. The diction, spelling, etc. of which I have preserved in the copy I now give to the public—

TO Mrs. K____ W____

MADAM

I dont understand your latter to me. I hav sid nothing to hurt your kar-ractter that I nose off—but I sall meet you at the time and place you mantion.

Your humbal servant,
G____ F____

Next morning I took my pistols and went to the appointed place half an hour before the time agreed upon. My antagonist was punctual to the hour.—Having approached me he enquired "what I wanted of him?" I smiled at his ignorance and pointed to my pistols. He said he did not understand me. I told him he must kill me or I must kill him. "Well," says he, taking off his coat, "will you have it rough and tumble, or will you box it?" Upon this he approached me—I told him to stand off or I would blow his brains out—he started as if he had seen Hamlet's Ghost,[22] and finding me seriously determined upon the duel he made concessions to me for his conduct. I demanded his certificate to be in writing, to which he acceeded. We went to Mr. Foster's, where I drew the following lines, which he subscribed without hesitation:

> "I acknowledge to have circulated a report implicating the reputation of K____ W____, representing her as improperly connected with the British government in Canada,—I certify that such report is mere fabrication, not having the least foundation in truth, but is wholly false and malicious—that I am sorry for my conduct, and make these public acknowledgments of my fault."

G____ F____

This affair be arranged to my satisfaction, I took my leave of Mr. Foster and family, and started for Albany where are arrived on the 11th day of March, in the year 1804.

∾≈∾

CHAPTER XI

Authoress' second journey into Canada and second interview with her husband, and its success . . . Prepares to leave Canada.

> Justice at last o'ertook him, and with her thunderbolts
> made him tremble—

ANON.[23]

NOT having heard from my attorney in Canada since I left it, I began to be impatient. I thought the least claim I had upon my husband was his duty to support me; and here I may remark, that too many females are lost to society by the inattention and cruelty of husbands, who, instead of benevolently aiding and giving them comfort, consign them to the bitter cup of poverty and distress. How many vices and crimes owe their birth to these causes! Man is perhaps worse from necessity than from choice—one deviation from virtue leads to another, till at last all sense of rectitude is extinguished.

On the 4th of May, 1804, I set off for Canada, and without material occurrence I arrived at Queenstown, where I have formerly been, and on my arrival wrote to my attorney the following note:

"The compliments of K ____ W ____ are addressed to R ____ S ____, requesting him to have the goodness to inform K ____ W ____ the result of the business committed to this charge last winter. She would be happy to receive his answer by the bearer."

Answer of R ____ S ____

"MADAM,

Agreeably to your directions I instituted a process against your husband shortly after your departure from Canada, and can only inform you that it is now in the state to admit of a certain decision at the next term in August, which I have no doubt will be favorable to your claims. I have barely to add, that your husband has signified to me a desire to have with you a second personal interview whenever he should understand that you have returned to this province, and that thro' me he wished to know whether (and what place and time) such interview would be agreeable to you.

> I am, madam, respectfully,
> Your very obd't serv't
> R ____ S ____
> Mrs. K ____ W ____

Authoress' Reply to R ____ S ____

"SIR,

Notwithstanding the request of S ____ W ____ (my false husband) ought in justice to my feelings not to be assented to, yet with a view to accelerate the desired object of my journey hither, I shall consent to his request. You may therefore inform him that I shall be at leisure to see him at the house of ____ (where I put up) to-morrow afternoon at three o'clock.

> I am, Sir,
> Your humble serv't,
> K ____ W ____
> R ____ S ____, Esq."

I had made up my mind to demand of S____ W____ my support only, and that he should give security for its punctual performance. Accordingly when he called at the hour appointed, I coolly informed him that if his object was to allow me a separate maintenance I would consent to hear whatever he proposed to state, otherwise I must decline any further correspondence with him. He assured me his object was to make me a decent settlement, and with that view only he had requested an interview. We were not long engaged in fixing the terms. He at once offered me a conveyance of a large and valuable tract of land in Canada which (after consulting my attorney) I consented to take. The deeds were draw on and executed that very day, and S____ W____ in addition to it supplied me with a handsome sum of money and some other articles. This business being arranged to my satisfaction, I prepared to leave Canada, and on the 2d June commenced my departure.

A long and last Adieu to my Husband.

SO fate has ordered, and I again must submit,
    That you and I no longer shall be one—
Then let us all our former love forget,
    And each the other henceforth strive to shun.

Where was my judgment, when you was my
        choice?
    Where was my reason, when I was so blind?
But thanks to Heaven! I'll once more rejoice,
    The fetters broken—they no longer bind.

Hence Hymen,[24] then, thy altar ne'er shall know
    Again a victim once deceived by thee;—
Here I proclaim aloud, "I am thy foe,"
    And death shall only end our enmity.
Adieu, to my husband once—no more the name
    Thrills thro' my soul with rapture or with joy;
Ah, the reverse—I'm fill'd with woe and shame,
    And peace again I never can enjoy.

CHAPTER XII

Authoress' return to Albany . . . Her imprisonment there for debt . . . She falls sick . . . The gaoler's benevolence towards her . . . Her discharge.

Alas! My lord, misfortune commenced with her
Very existence, and they followed her thro' life.

L. Bol.[25]

I ARRIVED on the 9th July, 1804, in the city of Albany, without any material accident by the way, intending immediately to start for Philadelphia, where a brother of mine resided, and at present an only brother. But many things fall out "between the cup and lip." So it proved with me—for on the 10th July the "grace of God," under "seal," was poured out upon me. My soul was ever "free and independent," and the littlenesses and persecutions of relentless creditors I despised the more they accumulated these persecutions. I was conveyed to gaol, having no other security to give but the deed of land I received in Canada from my husband, and which would not be accepted.—The idea of a gaol had already become familiar to my mind, and the face of a gaoler was no longer like the face of Medusa,[26] calculated to turn me into stone—It is true, into a stone-jug I was turned for my lodgings, and it was undoubtedly a disagreeable turn. But habit makes us little dread the evils of this world. Thanks to heavens, my gaoler was a *man*—had the feelings of a man—and the "milk of human kindness" had not yet curdled in his bosom from the duties of his office; every indulgence he could give, consistent with his duty, he extended towards me. On this occasion I penned the following lines:

THE BENEVOLENT GAOLER.

ROME has erected trophies to her sires,
        And raised triumphant arches to their fame;
Their memory thus preserved, no more expires
        And thus they gain a brilliant deathless name.
Yet he, who glows with genial warmth, whose
                breast
        Extends relief to woe where e'er its found,
Whose mind with mild benevolent is blest,
        In whom the softer virtues all abound:

He! who surrounded still by misery's walls,
    Whose eye beholds unceasing anguish roll,
Who ever bends an ear to misery's calls
    Which reach the inmost chambers of his soul.

He! whose kind hand shall ever give relief,
    And dry away the wretched captive's tear,
Whose kindness softens others moistened grief,
    Whose friendship as his bosom is sincere,

Dies! unremembered—scarce a stone proclaims
    The gloomy mansion of departed worth,
While kings and generals who've their thousands
    slain,
Are made the wonder and applause of earth.

Within the liberties of an Albany gaol I continued for several months, and my discharge was at length procured by the liberality of others. An indisposition followed immediately before my discharge which confined me to my bed for three months . . . Heaven at length restored me to my health but *poverty* was and *still* is my lot.

The preceding narration of my life may open a field of conjectures and conclusions. The serious incidents will, I trust, be justly appreciated by the cool and reflecting part of mankind; those of a novel and eccentric kind may perhaps distort the risible muscles of some, and I am aware it will meet censure and satire from many. Deficient in understanding, indeed, would be that person who appears in public thro a channel of this kind to calculate on universal applause and approbation. It is too much practiced both in speaking and writing to exert all the powers of the mind to insinuate ourselves to our readers by the aid of flowery fancy. This I have studied to avoid any farther than to narrate the incidences of my life and the feelings are rising from them, in the manner they occurred.

In my passage thro life thus far, I claim that I have never been in the habit (from a natural disposition and some share of education) of complaining or indulging myself in murmuring until I met with those crosses which I deem of the first magnitude; nor have I ever descended into invectives for the abuse and ingratitude I have experienced.

    The world my dear Myra is full of deceit,
    And friendship is a jewel we seldom do meet.

Friendship, as to its extent of operation and effects on society at large, and to individuals, is better felt than described; the cautious maxim of an eminent English author cannot be too much cultivated.

"Have but few friends but let them be sincere."

Happy is the possessor of such a maxim in its full enjoyment. But when we look around us and bring to our recollection how many, in their arrangement thro life, have, from fatal experience, built on false calculations, we lament the depravity of the world and shed tears for its treachery.

> "Happy in Paradise she lay,
> By a single act 'twas soon snatched away,
> Some ignus fatuua that leads astray,[27]
> And ruins many a woman every day:
> Whether within the flow'ry grove you hide,
> Or in the drawing room obtain the bride:
> Thou lewd pursuer of lascivious joy
> When no debauchery can ever cloy.
> Hang heavier with black, ye rivers stream with
>   blood,
> Reign vice triumphant e'er all that's good.
> Forked lightnings dart, ye murmuring thunders
>   rear,
> Seas burst your bounds and deluge every abore,
> Stars quit your orbs, and thou, all nursing sun,
> Beveiled, nor see thy daughter stain'd, undone.
> If love is of a celestial kind
> What grief, what horrors, doth it leave behind,
> A drop of sweets mixed with a sea of soures,
> They hate for ever who have lov'd for hours."

How happy then the situation of a person who has only one sincere friend. But how shall we paint the reverse; no doubt there are too many who feel the effects, verified by age and experience, and perhaps it has been my lot that I have in too many instances been an object of the reverse part of the picture of friendship and gratitude.

Thus in taking a retrospective survey of my former situation in life, when I view it in my crosses in a connected state; when I traced back my situation to a pecuniary and inconvenient point of view; when I seriously reflect on the novel and eccentric parts of my movements in life, that part is treated in my mind with more reflection (altho there is nothing criminal in it) than some may suppose who are acquainted with me.

And when I contrast my present precarious situation with my former part of life, it brings out forcibly to my mind, a sentiment, "It is pleasing to progress from old convenient situation, too lofty an affluent one."

But, to reverse the situation, nature and dispositions struggle hard; which feelings I have and do possess from sad experience and my immediate situation.

But in my solitary situation I call to my aid some of the sentiments contained in Zimmerman,[28] and from him collect all the reasoning I am capable of, and endeavor to adopt the maxim "be ye reconciled to your fate," and I hope I may and will profit by it.

FINIS.

NOTES

1. *Beware of yonder dog*—The correct quotation is from Shakespeare's *Richard III*, act I, scene iii, 297–302:

> O Buckingham! Take heed of yonder dog:
> Look, when he fawns, he bites; and when he bites,
> His venom tooth will rankle to the death.
> Have not to do with him, beware of him;
> Sin, death, and hell have set their marks on him;
> And all their ministers attend on him.

2. *Charming Susan*—Records show no ship with this name during this period. White had probably based this ship's name and the account of the storm on the story of another ship the *Charming Sally* (Arch 2001, 149–50; Bailyn 1986, 595–96).

3. *Genius*—Spirit; White is using an older meaning of genius, usually used in the plural form.

4. *Stockbridge*—Stockbridge, Mass., was established in 1736 by the General Court of Massachusetts Bay, and intended for the sole occupation and use of the Housatunnuck (Mahican) Indians and a handful of English families, whose presence would, it was hoped, encourage the "civilization" and conversion of the Indians. After the Seven Years War, the English population in the area grew rapidly and much of the Indians' land was sold or granted to the settlers. By 1774 the Indians had been effectively removed from active political participation in Stockbridge

affairs and owned a fraction of the original land grant. Although the tribe supported the American cause during the Revolution, the main body of the tribe moved in 1785 to New Stockbridge (Madison Co.), N.Y. (Frazier 1992; Miles 1994).

5. *From opening skies, may streaming glories shine*—The quotation is from Alexander Pope's (1688–1744) poem *Eloisa to Abelard* (lines 337–42):

> Then too, when fate shall thy fair frame destroy,
> (That cause of all my guilt, and all my joy)
> In trance ecstatic may thy pangs be drown'd,
> Bright clouds descend, and angels watch thee round,
> From op'ning skies may streaming glories shine,
> And saints embrace thee with a love like mine.

6. *Hymeneal rites*—Marriage rites; they derive their name from the Greek god Hymen (or Hymenaeus) the god of marriage. In Greek mythology, Hymen was often invoked to bless with his presence the nuptials (as in the story of Orpheus and Eurydice), but he does not necessarily bring with him happy omens (Flaum 1993).

7. *Wormwood and gall*—Wormwood and gall is a phrase derived from the Bible (Amos 6:12; Lamentations 3:19), used to refer to something extremely disagreeable. The wormwood plant (*artemisia absinthium*) is very bitter to taste and is said to trigger the release of secretions from the gallbladder.

8. *Morpheus and Mercury*—Morpheus was the Greek god of dreams. He lay on a bed in a cave, surrounded by poppies and was responsible for shaping dreams. Morpheus appeared to humans in their dreams as a man; he had the ability to assume the form of any human being and often appeared as a loved one in mortal dreams.

Hermes or Mercury (in Roman mythology) was the messenger of the gods and conductor of the souls to Hades. He was the god of travelers and roads, of luck, of music, of merchants and commerce, and of cheats and thieves. Although Hermes was responsible for good luck and wealth, he was a dangerous foe and a trickster (Flaum 1993).

9. *Misfortunes never come alone but in battalions*—the correct quotation is from Shakespeare's *Hamlet*, act IV, scene i (lines 75–78):

> O, this is the poison of deep grief; it springs
> All from her father's death, O Gertrude, Gertrude!
> When sorrows come, they come not single spies
> But in battalions.

10. *Compatency*—a living.

11. *Fortune, the sportive goddess*—The Roman goddess Fortuna was the daughter of Jupiter, in charge of fate (or luck) both good and bad. Roman emperors were

reputed to have slept with a golden statue of her in their quarters. She appears to have originally been a goddess of fertility (Flaum 1993).

12. *"Yes, truly,* . . . —White attributes this quotation to Shakespeare, but it does not appear in any of his works.

13. *Robed in justices'* . . . —This quotation, like other of White's anonymous quotes, may actually be her own. By attributing them to an anonymous author she can avoid being accused of leveling direct and open criticism. In this case she gets away with calling the men who sat in judgment of her "asses" or "justasses" (White, *Narrative,* XX) and their pronouncements "braying" (White, *Narrative,* XX).

14. *The nakedness of the land*—When Joseph's brothers came to Egypt in search of food Joseph falsely accused them of spying. "And Joseph remembered the dreams which he dreamed of them, and said unto them, Ye [are] spies; to see the nakedness of the land ye are come" (Genesis 42: 9).

15. *Mr. Catchpoll*—A catchpole was a term used for a sheriff's deputy, especially one who made arrests for default of debts.

16. *Wandering Jew*—In popular legend, the Wandering Jew was a Jew who mocked or mistreated Jesus while he was on his way to the cross, therefore the Jew was condemned to a life of wandering on earth until Judgment Day. This legend was first recorded in the chronicles of Roger of Wendover and Matthew of Paris (thirteenth century), but only in the early seventeenth century was the character identified as a Jew (see Hasan-Rokem and Dundes 1986).

17. *'Tis false* . . . —White was probably quoting from memory and referring not to Daphne but Daphnis. In the pastoral novel *Daphnis and Chloe* by Longus (circa the second century CE), Lamon is the name of Daphnis's adoptive father.

18. *Guardian genius*—see note to page 11.

19. *Say, should the fool's cap* . . . *Garrick*—White's partiality to quotes from plays by or attributed to the English actor and playwright David Garrick (1717–1779) is hardly surprising given that cross-dressing was a recurring theme in his plays. In *The Male-Coquette; or, Seventeen-Hundred Fifty-Seven* (1757), for example, two of the main characters engage in cross-dressing (Sophia disguises herself as a man and Tukley as a woman) in order to unmask the duplicity of another (Daffodil), who is pilloried for his effeminacy. Garrick is also known to have written the prologue to Hannah More's tragedy *Percy* (1778) in which he celebrated cross-dressing on the part of women (Fahrner 1993; Wahrman 1998).

Garrick also rewrote many Shakespearean plays for the stage, often adding and deleting scenes, tailoring them to his audiences' tastes. It is possible that White was quoting from these versions and not the original.

20. *Pope Joan*—The fable about a female pope, who bore the name of Johanna (Joan), first appeared in the middle of the thirteenth century. In this, the first ver-

sion, the alleged popess was a very talented woman who disguised herself as a man, advanced within the Church hierarchy, and finally became pope. One day when out on horseback, she went into labor and gave birth to a son. She was then stoned to death and buried where she died (see Boureau 2001).

21. *L. Bol.*—Given White's fondness of quotations from Shakespeare, she was probably referring to the character of Henry IV (1367–1413), who was known as Henry Bolingbroke before he ascended the throne. This quotation however does not appear in the three Shakespearean plays in which the character appears.

22. *Hamlet's ghost*—The conversation Hamlet has with his father's ghost (*Hamlet*, act 1, scene v) is the is the catalyst for action, as only then does Hamlet learn of his father's murder and begin plotting revenge.

23. *Justice*—Themis, the Greek goddess of divine justice, law, and oaths was one of Zeus's trusted and constant companions. She sat at his side whispering her advice to him. Themis herself was not associated with thunderbolts, Zeus was. In her later incarnation as the Roman goddess Justitia she was portrayed blindfolded, holding scales and a sword (Flaum 1993).

24. *Hymen*—see note 6.

25. *L. Bol.*—see note 21.

26. *Medusa*—Medusa was one of the three gorgons of Greek mythology. Once a beautiful woman, she offended Athena, who changed her hair into snakes and made her face so hideous that a glimpse would turn people into stone. Eventually the hero Perseus killed her and presented her head to Athena, but her head retained its petrifying power even after her death (Flaum 1993).

27. *Ignus fatuua*—Lat. *ignis fatuus*, foolish flame or delusive light (in this case, love).

28. *Zimmerman*—White was probably referring to Johann Georg Zimmerman, the Swiss-born doctor who became personal physician to King George III at Hanover. His essay, *Solitude Considered with Respect to Its Influence on the Mind and the Heart* (1793), was translated into several languages and published in America in 1806. *http://www.pbagalleries.com/catalogs/curcati133-6.html* (Site visited Oct. 10th, 2002).

MEMOIRS

of

MRS. ELIZABETH FISHER

of the

CITY OF NEW YORK

Daughter of the Rev. Harry Munro, who was a Chaplain in the British Army, during the American Revolution. – Giving a particular account of a variety of domestic misfortunes, and also of her trial, and cruel condemnation to the state's prison for six years, at the instance of her brother

PETER JAY MUNRO

WRITTEN BY HERSELF

Neither the perfidy of private friendship, nor the persecution of relatives, nor the frowns of the world, nor domestic calamity, nor time, nor circumstance, can shake the mind that is armed with conscious virtue.

New York
PRINTED FOR THE AUTHOR

THE REV. HARRY MUNRO, my father, was a native of Scotland.[1] After receiving his education, he was appointed Chaplain to the 77th regiment of foot,[2] commanded by General Montgomery,[3] and was sent to America at the conclusion of the war in the year '59. My father became acquainted with the widow of an officer who belonged to the same regiment; this widow became wife to my father and mother to me. I was born in Philadelphia, the second day of December, 1759; my mother died three days after my birth and left me to the care of my father, who soon procured a wet nurse for me in Burlington,[4] a quaker lady, with whom I remained until my father married a second time, and took up his residence in Princeton, New-Jersey. I was then taken home to my step-mother; I became very found of her, as she was fond of me, and soon forgot my nurse. Eleven months after her marriage she was delivered of a son. Some time after her recovery, my father took it into his head to go home to England to be ordained for the church of England, profering that to the church of Scotland. He took his leave, with intention of taking passage from New-York; but a few days after his departure from home, my step-mother was taken with a fit, and expired in a few minutes. A servant was sent off in haste to New-York to inform my father of what had happened; when the servant came to the ferry the wind was so high that the boat could not cross that night; the next day my father heard the melancholy news—the death of a woman whom he loved; it was customary in those days to bury the dead after candlelight; when my father came home, my mother's corpse was gone to the place of internment—I remember my father wept bitterly. The next day my nurse was sent for from Burlington, and my little brother and myself were given into her care. My father took his departure for England. A few months after my father's absence the nurse was alarmed by seeing the child in a fit; the doctor was sent for, but in vain, the child was soon a corpse. When my father arrived from London, and the nurse informed him of the death of his son, his feelings were deeply wounded. He left me in the care of the nurse and came to New-York, having letters of recommendation to Doctor Auchmuty,[5] then minister of the old Trinity Church;[6] he insisted on my father's making his home with him till some place should become vacant. Accordingly my father did so, and he frequently by invitation preached for the doctor, in several of the protestant churches in New-York. Preaching one Sunday in the old Trinity Church, by request of Doctor Auchmuty, a widow by the name of Chambers,[7] being one of the doctor's congregation, came to hear my father preach; she brought with her Miss Jay,[8] who was her niece; my father, being a handsome man, soon commanded the attention of that lady; he was often invited to dine at the widow Chambers, where Miss Jay first got acquainted with my father; she became very fond of him, although he was a stranger, and I have heard my father say that she was very unhappy when he was out of her sight. My father, being informed that Miss Jay was a lady of respectability and fortune, was advised by his friend, the doctor, to pay his addresses to her; which he did, and the marriage day was soon fixed on. They became man and wife; and, as all the family were pleased with the marriage, my father expected something handsome from her father, Mr. Peter Jay,[9] but he was much disappointed. Mr. Jay never gave him any thing excepting some furniture. Miss Jay was considerably advanced in years. Sometime after marriage, my father was appointed minister at Philips' Manor.[10] After they removed there, I was sent for. My nurse brought me home from Burlington, to my step-mother. The nurse stayed a few days with me, and then returned home to her family. I remember I fretted much after she left me, as my step-mother began to be very cross with me. When my father was from home, she would for the least misconduct, whip me, then lock me up in the cellar for a whole day, without giving me either victuals or drink. The servants would sometimes send me refreshments through the cellar window. Often in this situation I have cried myself to sleep; and whenever my father and she had any dispute she would revenge herself on me. When near her time, being ten months after marriage, she went to her fathers, who lived at Rye,[11] and took me with her, where I remained all winter under the care of her mother and sister, who were kind to me. On the tenth day of January, 1766, she was delivered of a son, who was baptized by my father a few days after his birth, and named Peter Jay Munro,[12] after his grandfather, he standing god-father for him. This event caused great joy in the family, as he was the first grandchild. In the spring, we all returned home, and it became my business to rock the cradle; he being very cross, I was frequently whipt because I could not quiet him. Her ill treatment of me was incessant, for I never was without marks of her cruelty; she would pinch me till my flesh turned black, and then lock me up in the cellar till I almost perished for want of food. I am confident that if the servants had been as destitute of feeling as she was, I must have died. My father and she soon began to live unhappy, he finding himself disappointed in getting a fortune by her; and what contributed to increase it, she was neither handsome nor agreeable in any respect whatever—of the most desperate temper, she possessed no qualification of a lady; the longer they lived together the more unhappy they seemed to be.

My father, having some words with Mr. Philips, removed from there to Albany. The cruelty of my step-mother still continued, until, at length, the neighbors informed my father of her conduct towards me. He forbid her correcting me, and told her, that if I needed correction, he would do it; but this admonition failed of success, for when ever he was from home, which was often the case, I would experience her cruelty in as great a degree as ever; at last, as nothing else would do, my father boarded me out, and sent me to school. The hard usage I had received from her, had such an effect on my constitution, that the doctor, believing me to be in a decline, advised my father to have me removed to the country.

My father had a patent of land granted to him for his services as a chaplain in the army; this entitled him to two thousand acres, which he drew in a place now called Hebron, in the county of Washington. As he wished to settle tenants on this patent, he went to this place in May 1775, and took me with him to spend the summer season. I had not been long there, before I perfectly recovered my health, and was much delighted with this change, being at liberty to range the woods as I pleased; my time was chiefly spent in seeking birds eggs, and catching little fish with a pin hook. My father provided a companion for me, a girl about my age, who went with me every where I pleased to go. The summer being passed, my father said to me one day, Betsy, my dear, we must think of going home to Albany, the winter is coming on, and if you are a good girl, you shall come here again next summer. We were at dinner when my father spoke these words to me. After he went out, I went to my bed and wept bitterly; to think of returning to my cruel step-mother, appeared to me worse in anticipation than death. I begged of my father to leave me in the country. I told him I did not wish to go home to my step-mother. My father seemed to hurt at my expressions, and said he would endeavour to get me board in a decent family, for the winter season, which he did. He was acquainted with a Mr. William Reid,[13] who lived in a place now called Salem, in the county of Washington. I went there to spend the winter; my father took his leave of me, saying he believed he could not see me again till spring, as he had business in Philadelphia, which would detain him some time there. I was perfectly happy, because I had not to return to my step-mother. On my father's road to Albany, he stopped at the house of a Scotch-man, by the name of Duncan Campbell,[14] here he remained some days, the weather being very stormy; during which, Mr. Campbell suggested his wishes to my father respecting his eldest son's paying his addresses to me,[15] to which my father consented. Mr. Campbell lived five miles from where I was boarding. In a few days after my father is taking his leave of me, I received a letter from him on this subject:

Argyle, November 7th, 1775

"My Dear Betsy,

The badness of the weather has prevented me from proceeding on my journey. I have taken these five days at Mr. Campbell's, but this day I shall take my departure from hence. My dear child, Mr. Campbell has requested the favour of me to consent that his son, Alexander Campbell; should pay his addresses to you; I have given my consent: now let me beg of you to receive

Mr. Campbell as a gentleman. I have likewise written to Mr. Reid, desiring him to pay every attention to him when he visits you.

Your affectionate Father,
HARRY MUNRO."

When Mr. Campbell paid his visit I was surprised that my father could consent to his coming to see me.—He was about six feet high, and forty-five years of age—no teeth, and gray hairs; of course, I could not like him. After a few visits he asked me to marry him. My answer was no. What does he do but go to Albany to see my father, in order to ask permission to make me his wife! though he failed of getting mine, he obtained my father's consent, and immediately bespoke his wedding clothes. He prevailed on my father to write me a letter, informing me what had been done. On his return he came to see me, and spent the afternoon; after tea we took a walk some distance from the house, when he told me he had a letter for me from my father, and took out his pocket book and gave it to me.—Anxious to return to my lodgings, to learn the contents of the letter, I excused myself, and went to my bed-room to read it.—The contents were as follows:

Albany, December 3d, 1775,

"My Dear Betsy,

"Mr. Alexander Campbell is here with me, and has asked my consent for you to be his wife; I have given my consent, providing his father will make over that part of his estate, that he now lives on, to his son, that in case of his son's death, his widow and children may have something to depend on; which request Mr. Campbell assures me, will be immediately complied with by his father; therefore my dear child as soon as this is done, I shall expect you to come to Albany with Mr. Campbell, to my house, to be joined in wedlock to a man whom I esteem as a good man and a gentleman; and if you refuse your consent, you must not expect forgiveness for me.

Your affectionate Father,
HARRY MUNRO."

When I received this letter, I was astonished at Mr. Campbell's conduct, to get my father's consent before he had obtained mine; as Mr. Campbell was the bearer of this letter, I read it in his presence, and my answer to him with this—"Sir, as you have courted my father, you may marry him, for I will never marry you." This soon came to my father's ears; I knew not what to do, I feared he would send for me home, which I dreaded—I was in great distress, knowing not what method to take to avoid the displeasure of my father, as I was very fond of him.—Sometime before I left Albany to go into the country my father had purchased two small lots of land about half a mile from the city of Albany, on one he built the store house, on the other is a dwelling house, where we lived. As I before mentioned, my father and step-mother lived very unhappy; they had separate beds for each other, which is a bad sign; her heart and soul were in her son. We had a large garden, and she was fond of spending her time in planting and transplanting. One day I remember she was setting out cabbage plants, and had set out a great number, she held the stick she made use of in setting them out in her hand, and began to count them, when her little son came behind her and began to count after her; this made her make a mistake several times in counting, she bid him be quiet several times, and he did not mind her, at last she got in a passion and knocked him down with the stick. As soon as he fell she called for the wench to come, and told her she was afraid she had killed her child; the wench took him up in her arms and carried him into the house and he soon recovered. That evening as he and his mother were sitting together, his mother was telling a story to the ser- vant maid concerning governor Colden hanging himself in his garden with his pocket handkerchief because he was in great trouble;[16] her little son Peter paid attention to her story; I have often seen him sit and look her in the face, and at the end of every sentence his little head would give a nod. The next day as he seemed to be very dull, she asked several times if he was sick, he said no; about twelve o'clock he went to the kitchen, and asked the wench to give him the small cord that hung in the kitchen; she asked him what he was going to do with it, he said he was going to play in the backyard. He took this cord and his little bench that he had to sit on (for he was a child of about six years of age) and went back of a wood pile that was in the back yard, in which was a piece of wood that stuck out far- ther than the others—he stood on his bench and tied one end of the cord to this stick and the other round his neck, then went on his knees by his little bench to pray—the wench, seeing what he was about, called his mother, and cord was taken off and he carried into the house—his mother was almost crazy; my father was from home. She asked him what made him try to hang himself; "why governor Osborn;[17] hung himself when he was in trouble, and I was going to hang myself, because you knocked me down in the garden yesterday." She was greatly alarmed for fear he would attempt it again. In a few days my father came home, and she informed him of what had happened, who said he ought to be corrected for such conduct—he called for him and whipt him for it; his mother was so angry because my father whipt him, that she said she would cut her throat with her penknife, but thinking better of the business, she only fell down in a fit, and was confined to her room for a few days.—My brother, from the time he was ten years old has been under the care of the Jay family, as they are his relations.

I had no relations.—I had to seek my living among strangers. In the month of January, 1776, Mr. Fisher became acquainted with me.[18] The first time I saw him was at a meeting.—Mr. Fisher been in the same regiment with my father, was very desirous of getting acquainted with me. He took his lodgings in the same house in which I boarded, where he was informed of what had passed concerning Mr. Campbell, my father, and myself. He made Mr. and Mrs. Reid his confidents and told them that he would reward them handsomely if they would endeavor to get me to consent to permit him to visit me; they soon by persuasion gained my consent to see Mr. Fisher. After he had been introduced by Mrs. Reid, she said that she and her husband had been acquainted with Mr. Fisher many years, that he was a good man, and a man of property, and would make a better husband to me than the man my father wished me to have.—Being young and inexperienced in life, I soon was made to believe that I should do well by marrying Mr. Fisher; I must confess I had no affection for him. The thoughts I had upon the subject were these: I shall have some one to take care of me—I shall have a home—I shall never be a trouble to my father, for surely he wants to be quit of me, or he would not have been so angry with me for refusing Mr. Campbell; and another thing which had great weight on my mind, was, that I should be out of my step-mother's power. After I gave consent to Mr. Fisher, I sent Mr. Reid to my father to acquaint him of Mr. Fisher's intentions towards me, and wished him to consent to our marriage, which he refused, and was much displeased with me. He sat down and wrote me a severe letter, as follows—

"BASE, UNWORTHY CHILD,

"What could tempt you to ruin yourself and break your father's heart? I never will consent to your marriage with Mr. Fisher for many reasons—he is too old for you, and he is no gentleman. If you take any rash steps, your blood be on your own head.—I will never own you as my child, or give you one shilling portion. I thought you was a girl of more good sense and a better spirit than to throw yourself away on the like of Mr. Fisher.

Your offended Father
HARRY MUNRO."
"To Miss Elizabeth Munro."

My father at the same time forbid Mr. Reid letting Mr. Fisher see me; but that was in vain, for we were engaged.—When Mr. Reid returned and informed me what had passed between him and my father concerning me, I was almost distracted. I loved my father, and wished to please him.—At one time I was for running away, at another for drowning myself; at last, however, I told Mr. Fisher, I could not marry him altho I had promised so to do. I then informed him of what had passed between Mr. Reid and my father, I likewise showed him my fathers letter to me. Mr. Fisher's feelings were hurt at my father's expressions against him; and he said he did not care for any portion of father could give; all he wanted was me, and my consent to be his wife; he would make over all his property to me, which was done. I considered for a few days what was best for me to do; I concluded to consent to marry him. Mr. Fisher went to New-York and got a license from governor Tryon,[19] and on the second day of February, 1776, I went with Mr. Fisher to Albany, and was married by Mr. Vesterlowe, a Dutch minister;[20] I never went to see my father, but returned with Mr. Fisher to the country. No one was present in our marriage but Squire McAlester who took us to Albany in his sleigh. Mr. Fisher then took me among his relations who resided on land that belonged to him. These people had the year before come from Scotland, some of them could not speak a word of English—here I was unhappy, but said nothing—sometimes Mr. Fisher would find me in tears, and wished to know the cause, but I would not tell the reason, for the reason was, I hated him and all his relations, for every thing they said and did was strange to me, and disagreeable. One day as I was walking in the wood, (for it was all wild, very little improvement having been made at that time, being new beginners,) I began to reflect on what I had done. I walked about a mile from the house, and sat myself down at the side of a large creek, where the water seemed to be deep; here I began to sum up all my troubles, and was fully determined to drown myself. I sat thinking and crying with my clothes unpinned, ready to jump in; the sun was near setting, I then lay myself down on the bank to rest, for I felt much fatigued, and instead of jumping into the creek, I fell asleep, with my gown turned over my head. I slept from sun down till ten o'clock at night, when I was surprised by Mr. Fisher raising me up in his arms, and asking me how I came there, and what I meant by going so far from home; I told him I had got lost; observing my clothes all loose, he asked me how they came so—to which I gave no direct answer. We went home; I slept but little that night, for I was very unhappy. The next morning he informed me, that when he came home the day before, he asked where I was, but no one could give any tidings of me, as the last that been seen of me was about three o'clock, walking in a field at some distance from the house; as night came on, my not appearing alarmed him very much—he went on the top of the house and blew the horn; but seeing no appearance of me, they at last set out to seek me, and came to the place where I was—it being dark, they saw something on the ground that looked black, and when they came up found it was me, fast asleep. When I awoke I did not know where I was.

We lived among Mr. Fisher's relations till the latter end of April, without hearing any thing from my father. A few days after the affair above related, I was standing at his brother's door, when Mr. Reid came and handed Mr. Fisher a letter to read; the letter was written to Mr. Reid, and the contents were these:—"Sir, I wish you to go to Mr. Fisher, and tell him to go to my patent and take his wife with him, and take possession of by house and farm and every thing that is there, as I am not satisfied that my daughter is living with his people." Mr. Fisher, remembering what had passed, was unwilling to go; he did not wish to be beholden to my father; but I was rejoiced at the news, and could not rest till he went with me there. I must say that Mr. Fisher was fond of me, and as I had lived there the summer before with my father, I thought it would seem like home to me; so we went there on the first of May. Mr. Fisher took with him his father, his half brother, and nephew and niece, and we had a boy of my father that was bound to him till he was of age—this constituted our family. The house was furnished and the farm stocked. As Mr. Fisher did not understand farming, all his business was left to other people. In June, as the people were mowing grass, Mr. Fisher having nothing to do, in order to amuse himself, gathered some small sticks which had fallen from the trees that stood near the barn, to which he set fire; it now being dinner time, the horn was blown for them to come.—While sitting at dinner, a smoke was observed coming round the house, they ran to the door, and, to their surprise, they saw the barn on fire; the barn was filled with wheat and hay of the year before. The fire, it seems, had been communicated from the brush Mr. Fisher had kindled, to the straw that was scattered around, and by that means conducted to the barn, and soon set it into a light blaze. They all ran to get out some calves that were confined, but could not; the barn was consumed in a few minutes.

So much for Mr. Fisher's work—We did not raise enough to support our family—we spent the summer gaining nothing. On the 14th of November, 1776, I was put to bed of a fine son.[21] During the winter I was confined to my room with a broken breast;[22] the child was very healthy. At this time Burgoyne[23] came down with his army to Skeensborough;[24] this put the country all in confusion; knowing not what to do, colonel Williams,[25] being a head man on this side of the country, came to Mr. Fisher, and begged of him, as he had been in the British army, to go and procure a protection for him and all the committee in Salem, and, he says, I will send John Baker with you,[26] that if you should be kept, Baker can return and inform us what is best to be done. Accordingly Mr. Fisher took his leave of his family, and went to see General Burgoyne; he made known his errand, and sent Baker back with the result to Colonel Williams. I expected Mr. Fisher home every day.

A few days after Baker's return, a party of riflemen surrounded our house, about six o'clock in the morning, and inquired for Mr. Fisher. I told them he was not home; they asked me where he was gone—I told them; upon which they ordered me out of my house, with the threat that if I did not immediately comply they would burn me in it. I took my child from the cradle and went out of the house.—I sat down at a little distance, and observed them taking out all my furniture, and then they burnt the house. In this situation, without a home and no one near me to whom I could apply for advice or assistance—not knowing where nor which way to go to find Mr. Fisher, I was at a loss what to do.—At last, seeing a man drive a cow, I asked him which way he was going.—He answered me to the camp.—I asked him if he would let me go along with him.—Yes, said he, if you can keep up with me. I arose from the ground (for I was sitting down with my child on my lap) and followed him. I walked that day, in company with this man, twenty-two miles, and carried my child; by the middle of the day I had neither shoes nor stockings on my feet; my shoes being made of silk, did not last long, and my stockings I took off and threw away, on account of the fatigue of caring my child and walking so far. I was willing to lay down and die. On the road this man would often say that he did not know but a party of Indians might be out a scouting, and if so, we should

fall sacrifice to them; at first I was alarmed, but my fatigue at length was
so great that I told him I wished they might come and kill me and my
child, for I was almost exhausted. I had nothing to eat or drink all that day,
except the water he gave me out of the brooks with his hat. We saw several houses, but the people had fled from them. About sunset we came to
a house where we found a woman and seven children. Her husband had
gone—I stayed there that night; the next day the man went with his cow
out into the camp; his cow was all he had, and he wanted to sell her for
money. I sent by him to Mr. Fisher, letting him know where I was. Mr.
Fisher came to me that evening, and the next day I went into the camp.
After I had been a few days in the camp I bought every thing my child and
I needed. I related to Mr. Fisher what had been done at home—he was
much surprised at Williams' conduct, as he had sent him and the men that
burnt the house were under his command—my furniture was sold at his
house as tory property. We then concluded to remain in the British army;
we stayed in the camp till Burgoyne capitulated. In October following, I
was eye witness to the death of General Frazer—I was in the same house
with him—I saw his death and burial.[27] After we were defeated we saw
hard times; provisions were scarce, and not to be had for money. I must
now give you some account of what passed from the time for our retreat
till the capitulation took place. We retreated after the last battle[28] to
Saratoga,[29] where we encamped at a small distance from the river, to prevent their cannon having any command over us—having nothing to do,
waiting for General Burgoyne's orders. We were deprived of all comforts of
life, and did not dare to kindle fire for fear we should be observed from the
other side of the river, and they may fire on us, which they did several
times. Being about the middle of October, we suffered cold and hunger;
many a day I had nothing but a piece of raw salt pork, a biscuit, and the
drink of water—poor living for a nurse. At this time I had my child at my
breast, being eleven months old. One day, weary of living in this manner,
I told some of the soldiers' wives if they would join me, I would find out a
way to get some provision cooked—seven of them joined me. I spoke to
some of the soldiers that were invalid, and told them if they would make
up a fire back in the wood, and get a large kettle hung on, we would fill it
with provision, and cook it, which would last us some time. They consented to do it for a guinea; they went to work and built up a fire, hung on
the kettle, and put water in it, then we women put in what we pleased; we
soon filled it with a variety; it began to boil; we all kept a distance from
the fire for fear of the cannon that were placed on the other side of the

river on a high hill; they soon discovered our fire, and saluted us with a cannon ball; it struck and it broke our kettle to pieces, and send the provision in the air. We met with no hurt only losing our intended feast. The soldiers demanded their pay, which I paid; but as the disappointment was so great, the rest declined paying anything, saying they had lost enough by losing their provision, so for my folly I had to pay for all.

A few days after the capitulation took place, when I saw the troops lay down their arms, I was glad, for I was wishing to get out of the camp. Mr. Fisher said he should go to Canada. I refused going with him, and went back to Hebron, where I meant to have stayed. Mr. Fisher proceeded on his way to Canada. On his arriving at Diamond Island,[30] he met my father, who asked for me. Mr. Fisher told him that I was not willing to go to Canada, at which my father was angry, and said he must go back and bring me and the child. Mr. Fisher came for me and told me what my father had said. I was surprised that my father should insist on my going to Canada, as I never had spoken a word to him since my marriage with Mr. Fisher. To please him I went, and when we got to Diamond Island my father was gone on his way. The next day we followed and overtook him at Monat Independent;[31] he was walking in company with General Powell.[32] When we landed, he came and took me by the hand and kissed me, and looking at my child, he asked me if I had named him, I told them I had not, you must, says he, call him after me. This was the first time I had seen or spoken to my father since my marriage; he likewise told me he would see me in Montreal. The next day we all set off to cross Lake Champlain; the season of the year being far advanced, and going to the northward, we found it very cold and stormy. We were eleven days on the lake, in an open boat, it snowed and rained every day; we slept on shore every night on the ground, as there were no inhabitants of on that side of the Lake in those days, for they had fled on account of the war. On the 22d day of November we landed in Montreal. As the river St. Lawrence was almost frozen over, we found it exceedingly cold.

I named my son *Harry Munro Fisher*. When we came to Montreal, we found the town very much crowded, and house-rent and fire wood high. As we had nothing to do, we hired some rooms and lived with a French family that winter; the next spring we bought a house and began business. My father boarded with Mr. John Thompson, a Scotchman; but as soon as he had got into comfortable lodgings he was taken very bad with a cold, and for six weeks we did not expect he would recover. I went every day to see him, and to do some little things for him. One day as I was combing his head, he asked me if Mr. Fisher had any money by him, I said he had; do you think, says he, Mr. Fisher would let me have some. I answered I did not know, but I would ask him. I told Mr. Fisher what my father said; well, says he, Betsy, you have my money in keeping, you may act your own pleasure with your father. The next day when I went to see my father, I told him Mr. Fisher was willing to let him have what he wanted; he said he would not want any till the spring, when he was going home to London. Several times he would ask me if I was contented with my husband; I always said yes; God knows I was not; but I was ashamed to confess to my father that I was exceedingly unhappy. On the first day of January, 1778, being New Year's day, I took my child and went to see my father. I stayed with him the greater part of the day; on coming away he put a guinea into the child's hand, and said he wished he was able to give something more. My father continued to be very much afflicted with sickness during all that winter. He would frequently ask me how Mr. Fisher was, but never invited him to see him. One day as we were sitting alone, he said to me, Betsy, you have made a bad choice in a husband; Mr. Fisher is old enough to be your father, and you must expect sooner or later to be left a widow, and perhaps with a family of small children, unprovided for. He often said to me I will endeavour to give you something before I leave you. I told this to Mr. Fisher. What can he give you, said Mr. Fisher, when he wants to borrow money to take him home. If he should offer you any money, continued Mr. Fisher, do not take it; you do not want it, for we can help ourselves. Not long after my father said to me, Betsy, I intend to give you a deed of my patent of land, for you and your children, in case you should become a widow, that you may have something to depend on. I told him I did not want it; for Mr. Fisher had forbid me accepting any thing from him, as we did not stand in need. It is not to Mr. Fisher I mean to give it, it is to you and your children. I shall give it to you before I go, but I wish you to say nothing about it to him. I will also leave you my servant boy, he can wait on your child—which he did. On the 12th day of February, 1778, he gave me a deed of his patent, telling me to take care of it, but never to say any thing concerning it till after his head was laid in the grave. I took it, but thought no more of it than I would of a piece of blank paper. The 6th of May as he was going to Quebec, on his way to London, he came to see me, and drank tea with Mr. Fisher and myself. Mr. Fisher asked him if he wanted some money, he said yes, he wished to have what he could spare, and asked what business we meant to follow. Mr. Fisher told him he intended to import goods the next year. Well, says my father, you may send your orders home to me, and you shall have your goods sent you; he then took what cash he wanted, for which he gave a note, and then took leave of us. That year we bought a house, and sent an order home to my father for goods. When the shipping arrived, there were no goods, not even a letter, from which we concluded that the old gentleman was dead. The year following we got Mr. William Aird,[33] a Scotch merchant, to import goods for us, paying ten per cent commission; the goods came, and every year after that we got our goods from him. We heard not a word from my father from the time he went home, which was in the year '78, till '86.

We remained in Montreal and did business to great advantage; but I was still unhappy, for as my husband advanced in years, his temper grew peevish, and he was very unhappy. I often ask him what was the cause of his unhappiness; and he said that when he looked at me and his dear little children, he was almost distracted, knowing he must soon leave us; and at the same time made this observation, that if he could be so fortunate as to leave us independent, he would die happy. He now began to neglect his business, thinking he could make more money by buying and selling lands. At this time I was mother of four children, two sons and two daughters. I endeavoured to discourage Mr. Fisher from his intended proceedings. In the year 1786, a gentleman by the name of Covel, who was a captain in the British army, called on me and told me he had just arrived from London, where he had seen my father, and had dined with him several times; he told me that my father had given him a letter to deliver to me with his own hand, which he did. I was happy in hearing that my father was living, although his conduct was not so pleasing as I wished. When the captain went away I open my letter and read it. The contents were these: he informed me of his having put in his claim to government for his losses in America, wishing me to procure the affidavits of three respectable men, who were acquainted with his landed property in America. I got Mr. Alexander Campbell, my once intended husband by my father, and Mr. James Campbell,[34] his brother, and Alexander Fisher,[35] those three men, being acquainted with the land, went before Judge Frazer,[36] of Montreal, and appraised the 2,000 acres of land on oath, at 5 dols. per acre; this being done, I enclosed the affidavits in a letter to my father, which he received. He made no apology in his letter for not writing to us before, and I never asked him the reason why he did not, but it caused me many a tear.

In the month of February, '87, Col. Jessup[37] came from London to Montreal, and brought me a letter from my father, wherein he acknowledged the receipt of my letter and the affidavits I had enclosed to him, observing that they came to hand in good time, and said that he had received compensation from government for his losses in America, in three dividends; desiring me to remember whose daughter I was, and at his death I should have something handsome. At this time I was mother of five children, two sons and three daughters. Mr. Fisher at this time was fully determined to quit business, and become a land speculator. In March, 1788, he left Montreal, and went home to England to purchase land from one David Milligan, who had landed in Washington county, state of New-York; he purchased those lands and returned to America the year following. He then left Montreal and resided in the United States where his lands were and left me in Montreal with my small family to shift for myself. My trial was hard, for he left me no support when he went away, excepting some outstanding debts for me to collect, which came in very slow, he being absent, and I only a woman. He took all the cash that was in the house with him. After three years absence he wrote me a letter, desiring me to come and bring the children with me, as he had a good home for us; accordingly I sold all off and went to him, expecting to find every thing ready for my reception; but great was my disappointment when I arrived and found him living with his sister in a small log house; instead of having a home, I was obliged to hire two rooms of a Mr. Smith, for myself and my family; there I remained one year. I took with me plenty of clothing and provisions. Seeing myself unprovided for, I repented that I had broke up house-keeping, and was determined to return to Montreal and try to get a living for myself and children. When Mr. Fisher found it was my wish to return, he and his sister's children took every thing from me, even my clothing, and I had to make my escape by night. After this I never lived with Mr. Fisher as a wife. When I returned to Canada I hired a house and took in work for a living, as I had nothing else to depend on. My father and brother paid no attention to my wants; my eldest son being now sixteen years of age, and having all the education that I could give him, I bound him to Mr. Isaac Todd,[38] a merchant, who took him to the country, where he is now married to his second wife, and is father of five children. I am informed that he is a man of handsome interest. My youngest son continued at school, and my daughter I kept at home. I found I could not support myself and family in a city by industry, and having lived a few years before in the state of affluence, I could not bear the idea of staying in Montreal; and to return to Mr. Fisher I would not. I spent days and nights thinking what I should do, and at last concluded to go to Hebron and live on my father's patent, as I thought I could do better in a country place. I left Montreal and went there; when I came there I made a bargain with Daniel Plumley for his house and farms, for three hundred pounds; this was for his improvements, as I thought the soil was mine. I came there the ninth of March, 1798; the twenty-first of September following, Mr. Fisher, after a few days illness, departed this life. On his death bed I visited him frequently; he seemed hurt to think he had behaved to me in the manner I have related, but said it was the fault of his relations; they advised him to it; he hoped I would forgive him. After his death I seemed to be more reconciled, for he was a great trouble to me when living. My daughter Eliza and myself lived together very happy.

Without observing the order of time, I must go back and relate some circumstances which may not be uninteresting to the public. I first thought it best to omit them; but as they tend to fill some chasms in the foregoing narrative, and as it is my object to give a correct outline of my history, I will here relate them.

In the year '90, I received a letter from Mr. Fisher to meet him at Caldwell's Manor on Lake Champlain,[39] in which he desired me to bring the children with me to see him. I took my children and a negro girl to wait us, and went to see Mr. Fisher. After staying there a week, I thought it time to return, as we had to put up at his half brother's, who was a poor man. The next day I hired a sleigh to take us home. When he saw I was determined to go, he took my negro girl and sold her to one Joseph Mott,[40] for seventy pounds, who took her to his house. I thought hard of Mr. Fisher's conduct towards me, knowing that I had our children to take care of. I took my children and set off for home. As I was riding along, and formed a plan which I was determined to put in execution. I ordered the driver to stop at a Mr. Duer's,[41] which was about eight miles from the British lines. I delivered my children, my pocket-book with papers, and my money, excepting what I might want, to Mr. and Mrs. Duer, and told them, that if anything should happen to me, to send my children and property to Mr. Fisher at Montreal,[42] who was a nephew to my husband; they promised they would. The children were put to bed, and knowing nothing of my departure fell asleep. I ordered the sleigh to be in readiness, and borrowed a great coat and fur cap of John Lockard Wiseman, and set off with a full intent to "conquer or die." I told the man what I was going to do, and desired him not to expose himself, as I should act as I thought proper. We set off from Mr. Duer's about eight o'clock in the evening, and rode on the lake as the ice was good. On passing Wind-Mill Point,[43] we observed a number of people in the tavern. I wanted to know if Mr. Fisher or Mr. Mott were to be there; accordingly I left the sleigh on the ice, walked in the house, and called for a glass of gin; while there I had a full view of the company. I knew them—neither Mr. Fisher nor Mr. Mott were there; but I was informed at this place that Mr. Fisher had taken the wench from his wife and sold her to Mr. Mott, and that he had gone to Mr. Mott's to stay till he should return to the States. I was pleased at this information, and went on in pursuit of the negro girl who loved me beyond expression. I arrived at Mr. Mott about two o'clock in the morning; I then ordered the driver to turn the sleigh, and be ready to start as soon as the girl got into it. I walked up to the house, and knocked at the door—no one answered. I took hold of a string opened the door, and went in. Mr. Fisher was lying in bed, and the girl before the fire on the floor. When Jane saw me she got out and began to cry. I whispered her to be quiet. Mr. Fisher awoke, and got up, saying he well knew my business, but I should find myself mistaken. You want Jane, he said, but shall not have her, for I have sold her to Mr. Mott. I spoke very little. All the family got up while Jane was making the fire; I told her to jump into the sleigh; she took the hint, and went out of the door; seeing the sleigh, she got in, when they went off and left me setting by the fire. Hearing the sleigh make a noise on the ice, and missing Jane, everyone ran to the stable for a horse, and galloped after it. They overtook the sleigh and brought it back to a tavern; they beat the man almost to death, took the sleigh from him, and made him a prisoner. This tavern was about two miles from the place were I found Jane. I saw them return and pass by. Unable to procure a sleigh, I set out on foot, and arrived at the tavern at about day-light. I found the man lying on a bench, the girl was confined in the house, and the horses the sleigh locked up in the stable. I spoke to Mr. Gregor (for that was the man's name who owned the horses and sleigh) and told him not to go to sleep, but to lie still until I should give the signal for him to be ready. He did so; I went into the bar-room where a large company had assembled to hear the news. When Mr. Fisher saw me there he said to me, "Well, Madam, you thought you would get Jane, but you shall not; I will let you know that I am your master; and as for Mr. Gregor, he shall go to jail, and lose his sleigh and horses." I said a little, but thought a great deal.

I saw they were all drinking very freely, and Mr. Fisher by this time being under full sail, I called for egg-nog, insisting on the company to drink, as I had lost, it was my treat, for they had had a great deal of trouble with me all night. About eight o'clock in the morning they all felt fatigued, and went to take a nap—no sleep was near me. When all were at rest, I called the landlord and asked him what I had to pay; after he told me that I had paid him. I then asked him to walk out with me; he went with me out of the house, when I informed him what had happened during the night, told him that I wanted him to go to bed, and permit me to take the sleigh and horses out of his barn, and my wench out of his garret, and make my escape. If you will comply, said I, you shall be well paid for it. I then put two half-joes into his hand, and he went to bed. I went to the man and desired him to go to the barn and fix his sleigh and horses as quickly as possible. While he was doing this, I went into the garret and awoke the wench; the sleigh being ready, the wench and myself jumped in, and away we went; we never stopped till we came to Mr. Duer's house where I had left my children the day before. When we arrived there it was three o'clock in the afternoon. Mrs. Duer got tea for us. I paid her for her trouble, returned my borrowed coat and cap to Mr. Wiseman, took my children and proceeded on my journey to the Isle of Noah,[44] where we spent that night, being then out of danger. The next day we arrived home in Montreal. I paid Mr. Gregor for his trouble, and he returned home to his family. I was determined this should be my last visit to Mr. Fisher, unless I could go alone.

Sometime after this I was washing some things for the use of my family, and sent Jane to a grocery to buy me some starch; on her way she was taken by an officer, and carried to prison, as being the property of the person to whom Mr. Fisher had sold her. I thought the girl stayed a long time with the starch, and sent after her; I was told that she had been put in jail. This surprised me, because I knew not what it could be for. As the officer was taking her across the parade, my eldest son, passing by, and seeing Jane in his custody, concluded to follow them. Jane was left below while the officer went up stairs to make his report—my son bid her run home, which she did. When I got up (for I was so much over-come, with trouble that I had lain down on the bed to reflect on my unhappy fate) I saw Jane coming in at the back gate; she told me what had happened. I then sent her away from me until such time as I could get a master for her. A few days afterwards I sold her to one Simon Clark in Montreal for thirty pounds, and gave him a bill of sale of her.

This wench was made a present to me by my step mother, in the year '85, when she was about six years of age. I know not whether my conduct, in accepting this wench, will be received with approbation by the public; but as I wish to give the correct account of all I can recollect, nothing shall be intentionally omitted, whether it be for or against me.

In this year ['85] I came from Montreal to New-York to see my brother,[45] after his return from England, where he had been with his uncle, John Jay.[46]

I found him at Bedford, studying law with John Strong, Esq.;[47] he was then a lad of about nineteen years of age. I was happy to see him. The Jay family all treated me very well; even my step-mother seemed happy to see, and made many inquiries after my father. She wished me to write to him, and beg him to write to her, "for," she said, "I have frequently written to him, but have received no answer, which makes me very unhappy." I promised her I would.

I spent the winter in New-York. On my return in the spring, I wrote to my father and informed him of my visit to New-York, and how kindly I was received by Mr. Jay's family; what a promising youth my brother was, and how happy I was in seeing him. I likewise informed him how desirous my stepmother was that he should write to her; and observed that she was sensible of her ill conduct towards me when under her care; how she had confessed that her conscience upon reflection made her very unhappy, and begged my forgiveness, saying, that if I could forgive her, she would die in peace. I forgave her, and begged of my father also to forgive her. Upon which he wrote to me in the following manner:[48]

"My Dear Betsy.

"You write to me that you have been to New-York to see your brother and the Jay family. I am surprised that you can write or correspond with a family that has abused your father in the manner they have done. My wish is that you will have nothing to say to any of them. I never will write to Mrs. Munro for many reasons, and I wish you not to make mention of her in your letters to me. I thought you had a better spirit than to wish to correspond with your father's bitter enemies."

I confess my feelings were hurt at his letter. I thought he was cruel towards his wife, but did not understand the cause; I knew they did not live happy when together. After that, when I wrote I never made mention of any of that family, for fear of hurting his feelings.

I must to give my readers some account of my conduct during the time I lived with my step-mother, she being so cruel, I was always on my watch to do her all the mischief I could. She had a parrot that she used to learn to tell every thing that passed when she was gone from home. One day our hired women expected company to drink tea—they went into the cellar and took butter and flour to make some cake—Poll was very quiet—they drank tea and went away; some of the cake being left, they put it in a basket and hung it up in the kitchen—my mother came home, and went into the kitchen, when Poll began to talk, "cake, basket—cake, basket mistress." My mother went and took down the basket, and found the cake, for which the servants got a severe reprimand. I had been playing in the yard, and with a stone I knocked over one of her little bantun [bantam] hens. I was for throwing it into the necessary, but the servants requested me to give it to them—they threw it into the oven. When my mother was done scolding about the cake, Poll cried out "oven—chicken—oven—chicken." She opened the oven and found the fowl—she began to inquire how it came there; they told her that as I was playing in the garden I went to drive out the hen and by accident hit it with the stone and killed it, they had taken it to cook. I was called for; nothing would excuse me from a whipping, and I got it severely. I was determined from that moment to be the death of the parrot, when the opportunity would serve.

One evening as my mother had gone out to supper, I was trying to discover some method to kill the parrot without its coming to the knowledge of the servants; at length I hit upon one, which was, to give her a fat meat with salt on it. When my mother came home, the parrot was sick, and in the morning she died—at this I secretly rejoiced.

Every summer my step-mother and her son went to New-York, to see their relations—I was always left home. When they returned, they would bring home birds, dogs and many other things to amuse themselves with. At one time they brought home a slut of which she was very fond;[49] the slut by her orders, slept in the entry every night, and if she made any dirt, it was my business to clean after her; I at length got very tired of this employment, and was determined, if possible, to put an end to her life.

One morning, my step-mother got up earlier than usual, and found my morning's work unfinished, for which she gave me a whipping; the same evening I saw an old carman that I knew,[50] to whom I made my complaint; he told me he would assist me in getting rid of the slut—accordingly, that night, it being moon-light he came and got the slut to follow him—he took her some distance from the house, and killed her. Great inquiry was made after the slut, and a reward offered, but she never appeared; so my labour in this business ended to my great satisfaction.

We had another dog for my brother's pleasure. This one I had to feed, and when lost, to find him. One day Penny, (for that was his name) was missing. I was told to look for him, but as I could not find him, I did not dare to go home; what to do in this predicament, I knew not, but was fully bent on killing the dog if I should find him. At last the dog came home, which occasioned great joy with mother and son, but not with me, for I yet felt the smart of the whipping I received for not finding him. That night, when my brother was asleep, I drowned the dog. The next morning I was sent again to look for him, *but could not find him*. I told a little boy where he was, and desired him to go and tell the news, which he did; the dog was carried home and decently buried.

My mother was a woman who thought that if the dogs barked at night, some one was coming to rob her. She slept up stairs by herself; whenever the dogs began to bark, she would open the window, a clap hands and cry out "catch him, Cloe! Catch him, Cloe!" This was her slut's name. One night as I lay in bed, I thought I would do something to frighten the old lady; so just before day I got up and took the key of the store-house, and opened the doors and windows—I upset everything I was able to lift and threw several pieces of meat out of the door and window. I left them open, hung up the key in the same place where I got it, and went to bed again, watching the motions of my mother. A little after day, she got up and looked over towards the store-house, and saw the door and windows all open—she ran down in her chemise, and told my father this door was broken open, and robbed of every thing; over they both went, with very little clothing on them, for they were in too great a hurry to put on any. They saw pork and beef laying outside the door; after taking a thorough view, they returned to the house, and calculated their loss—by their account, they had lost a great deal, but in fact they did not lose the value of a cent. After breakfast my father went and ordered the printers to put up advertisements through the town and offered five pounds reward for the thief; he then went to the blacksmith's and ordered him to put up iron bars across the door and windows, but no thief was discovered. I would often ask my father if he had found out the thief: No, child, he said, I wish I could. I had a mind to tell him it was me, but was afraid of making him angry. He never knew who it was. I did it to vex my mother; but was sorry for my father.

In the year '89 having business in the states, I left Montreal and crossed Lake Champlain. On my arrival, Mr. Fisher, who was there at the time, came to the landing to see me; at our meeting he was introduced to a young man who had lived in my house in the capacity of a merchant. Mr. Fisher gave this gentleman an invitation to his house to spend a few days, which he did. After some days it passed, I perceived by Mr. Fisher's discourse that he was unhappy on account of this man's having been in company with me on board of the vessel. He was advised by his nephew to ask this man, if he was willing to be qualified before a justice, that he had no criminal connexion with me during the passage over the lake. The young man, was surprised at this request, but consented to give every satisfaction in his power to appease the mind of Mr. Fisher. 'Squire Shelden was the man sent for to do the business. I was present. After the young man had taken his oath, these questions were put to him: Did you ever, at home or abroad, have any errant knowledge of my wife? He replied no. In my absence, as you boarded in the house, did you ever see any man pay attention to my wife in a criminal way? No sir, I never did. He was asked many more questions of the same nature, till he and his nephew were satisfied. The 'squire got his dollar for administering the oath, and returned home leaving us to think what we pleased on this subject. As for my part, I cannot express my feelings. The young man asked Mr. Fisher if he was satisfied; Mr. Fisher said yes. He then proceeded on his journey to Boston. After he was gone, I asked Mr. Fisher what he meant by such conduct—if he and I had any knowledge of each other, I said, do you think he would confess it—or do you think I would? No, my dear man, I never would; and for what has passed, you and I must bid adieu to each other. It may well be conjectured, how unhappy I felt on this occasion. I was bent on going home as soon as possible, never to return more. After my return home I met with more trouble. I left White-Hall with capt. Gilbert—we had three passengers besides myself. We set sail with a fair wind, and arrived at Burlington about sunset. Our boat being nothing but a small barge, we concluded to stay at Burlington that night. We supped and spoke for lodgings; but the captain ordered us on board again by ten o'clock that night; there being no woman on board but myself, I refused going but the captain insisted so hard upon our going that we all consented and went on board. By this time the wind was very high; the captain said however there was no danger. When we got into the bay, which is very wide, (I think twenty-two miles) it was midnight, and every one had to take his turn at the pump. The captain having liquor on board, drank so freely that he lost his way. At three o'clock in the morning we found ourselves at the lower end of the bay, among the rocks, expecting every instant to go to the bottom—at last we struck, and immediately filled with water. By jumping overboard, and getting on the rocks, we were saved from being drowned. When day appeared, we sat on a high rock, and saw at a distance the canoe—we hoisted a signal of distress, which was my white pocket handkerchief, that being all we had left, having lost in the storm the whole of our baggage, excepting a small box of papers belonging to Captain Grant who was in Montreal,[51] which had drifted on shore. We were taken off the rock and put

ashore five miles from Cumberton Head,[52] where we had to go for breakfast—wet and wearied as we were, those five miles we had to walk through
a wood, and only on a foot path. We reached there about ten o'clock in the
morning, and got some refreshments. The man went in search of another
boat, and I went to bed and slept till five o'clock in the evening; then I got
up and went on board, when we sailed for St. Johns,[53] where I thought myself
at home. The next day I took the stage for Montreal.

Having left my eldest daughter with her father in the country, on
account of her ill health, she being a weekly [weakly] child, I was very anxious to go and bring her home; the ice being good; and plenty of snow. I
took a sleigh and went for her. When I came there, I found her very sick;
after staying there ten days she died. When Mr. Fisher saw me going to
return, he forbade the man taking me with him.—I insisted on going, and
go I did. We went about eight miles, when an officer stopped us and made
us prisoners, and bound us over to appear at court. I had to give bail to the
amount of five hundred pounds for the man. The court sat the next day,
and a great crowd of people were gathered to hear the trial. The man was
charged with taking me away, being the wife of Mr. Fisher, and with having Mr. Fisher's property with him—Mr. Fisher was present with his
nephew—I plead my own cause, and likewise the man's, who was almost
frightened to death, for fear he should lose his horses and sleigh. The court
opened about six o'clock in the evening, and dismissed us about ten
o'clock that night. I gained the cause, and took my departure from thence
for Montreal.

By these trials it may be seen what I suffered in a married state.—What
I have gone through since the death of Mr. Fisher, the following will show.

In the year 1800 I was advised to try the virtue of the deed I had in
my possession for many years. I sent for a lawyer and took his advice,
which was to serve writs of ejectment on two or three of the tenants, and
that would settle the validity of the title. I did so; the tenants that were on
the land held a lease from my brother, Peter Jay Munro, as their landlord.
On my brother's hearing what I had done, he came up to Hebron in company with Samuel Young;[54] he did not stop at my house, but rode past, and
put up at a Mr. Daniels. The day after his arrival he sent Mr. Young to my
house to ask me to come to Mr. Daniels to speak with him. I told Young I
would not—that if Mr. Munro had any business with me, I was at home,
and he might come and see me. He came, accompanied by Mr. Young, and
after sitting a few minutes, asked me what I had been about. I told him I
wished to try titles with him. He asked me if I was willing to show the

deed; I said yes, and went to my trunk, and gave him the deed to read. He asked me concerning the witnesses. I gave him every information in my power who they were, and where they lived. My brother went with Mr. Young to his house. The next day he came again and asked me many questions. I gave every information in my power. A few days after this he made some proposals to me, which I rejected, thinking he wanted to take advantage of me. I knew at the same time that my father had given him a quit-claim of the same property I held a deed of.[55] He went away much displeased with me.

After my brother parted with me in Hebron, he went to Albany, entered a complaint, and had me taken prisoner and carried to Albany jail, where I remained from the 27th of October, till the ninth of March, and which time I was tried upon a charge of forgery—and a man by the name of John Nira Smith, to my utter astonishment, swore that he saw the deed executed in Ruport,[56] in the State of Vermont, by Adonijah Crane.[57] This evidence, being so pointed, I was sentenced to the state's prison for life. In a few days I left Albany and came to the New-York state's prison, and arrived on the 19th of March, but could not believe that I was to be a prisoner till I found the keys turned on me. I thought my brother could not be so cruel as to imprison a poor widow woman, who had suffered every thing but death, by having a cruel step-mother, a disagreeable partner in life, and left to an unfeeling and unpitying world, with three children, to do the best I could for a living. Such thoughts made me think my brother would be merciful. But no, his heart was unattached with mercy— I was to be immured in prison for life. Caring not for a life thus devoted I behaved very bad for a few days, for my wish was that they should punish me with death. I went in on Friday. On Monday the inspectors thought proper to place some confidence in me—they put the women prisoners under my command, which command I received with reluctance, but was pleased, nevertheless, with this mark of distinction. I should be wanting in my duty, if I passed by, without making known to the public the attention with which I was treated—they seemed to try to make me happy. After I had received my orders from Thomas Eddy[58] and John Murray,[59] I was desired by them to make a choice of room for myself, and a person to attend me. My provisions were sent me from the head keeper's table. I lived well, and was used well in every respect; but still, in the solemn midnight hour, when all my family were sleeping, instead of taking rest, I would walk the lonely hall, and viewed those dreary cells where in I was confined from the world—and for what, I knew not. Often at such times did I read the story of Joseph in the Bible, it being so similar to mine. After I had taken charge of these poor wretches, I called them all together in a large room, and spoke to them in this manner:

"Fellow Prisoners,

"As fate has decreed that I am to be one of this unhappy family, and the commanders of this place having thought proper to appoint me an assistant keeper, my sincere wish is that you will endeavour to obey their orders in every respect; and in obeying their's you will obey mine, for I shall require nothing from you that will be contrary to their orders to me; and by this method you will obtain their goodwill, and the goodwill of a woman who will have your welfare at heart, and will make it her study to make every thing as agreeable to you as this place will allow, hoping your conduct may be such, that when ever I am called upon to make a report, it may be favorable. My rules I will lay down before you, and you must be governed by them. If you refuse, I shall be obliged to compel you to submit."

I then took my station, and every thing went on very quiet; they were very fond of me, yet feared me, and never refused doing what I ordered them to do. I had the privilege of walking in the yard and garden, which made my time pass more agreeably. I enjoyed good health during my confinement, which was from the 19th of March, 1801, till the third of June, 1806. Gov. Lewis then thought proper to sign a pardon, and set me at liberty.[60] I parted from my family with sorrow, because I was going to leave them in confinement. During my imprisonment, my conduct met with universal approbation. I heard no complaints, and parted with them in friendship. After delivering every thing I had in charge, I took my leave, and went before the inspector, who gave me ten dollars. I am not mistress of language to express my feelings on going out of the gate. I came out alone.—I knew no person; I did not even know the way to town and was altogether a loss what to do. I felt nearly as bad coming out, as I did going in. I met with a friend who lived a small distance from the prison; he took me to his house, and made me welcome, till I could better myself. The next day I went to town to see my brother, but he refused to speak to me. I lived at this friend's house two months—during which time I had an offer of marriage from a man that I am sure would have made me a good husband; but I had no affection for him, and for that reason I would not have him. I knew what it was to marry a man one does not love. After two months I hired two rooms in the city, and took in needle work of all kinds, and worked late and early to get a living. I made out to live decently. I kept no help. During the last four years I have written many letters to people who were under many obligations to me in former days, relating my situation, but to my great surprise, received no answer, which makes the old proverb true "prosperity makes friends, and adversity tries them." I have now been four years from prison; my brother has never stept forward to assist me in any shape, and my children seem to have forgotten that I am their mother. Since my confinement, I have suffered many an hour of affliction in seeing my children possess such unnatural dispositions towards me, who go any lengths to serve them. Till now, I have been frequently asked why I did not try to make friends with my brother? I will leave it to himself if I have not condescend to the utmost to accomplish it; but nothing will do—I must set out with the resolution to gain a living for myself, and think no more of brother nor children. Hard is the task, but I am determined to do it. I believe the public in general will say that I have stood my trials through life with great fortitude. I feel for my brother, for I am sure he cannot be a happy man. I am sure, on reflection, he must feel hurt. He is father of a family; he must feel for his children; so must I, when torn from them and cast into a prison to drag out a miserable existence, forever a disgrace to myself and children. He must feel wretched on recollecting that it adds neither credit to himself nor to his family. I am his sister, and he cannot deny it. I am the only sister he ever had. My father, I hope, is in heaven; but I cannot avoid reprehending his conduct to me while living. To say one thing to me, and to say and do another, quite contrary, to my brother—writing to me not to correspond with my brother, nor any of the Jay family, saying they were his enemies, and at the same time corresponding with them himself, is conduct that cannot be justified; it has been, I believe, the whole cause of my brother's going to such extremities with regard to the property; but as he was a man of fortune, there surely was no necessity of practicing upon me so much cruelty. If this world was offered to me to make me treat him as he has me, I would not do it. What is property? It is only lent, and we must soon leave it; then we shall no more contend who shall have the most—no state's prison to be sent to if we cannot agree—no false witnesses to swear against us. I never blamed the judge for my sentence, for the evidence was so pointed against me that they could not do otherwise. I have been told by a gentleman in this town, that if I would behave myself, my brother would not see me want for anything. I wish I knew what kind of behaviour he wishes. I have been four years living in New-York, and I defy any person to say any thing that is disrespectful of my conduct. I have always lived in a decent neighbourhood, my conduct must be known by them, and by them I am willing to be judged. I want nothing from him, and if I did I do not think I should get it; for I know his heart; I have full experience of his *good will* towards me and my family; my innocent children feel the smart of his conduct more than I do at this present time—for I am advanced in years—it matters no great with me which way things go while I remain. But my children, just stepping on the stage of life, to have such a slur of character on them as to be told—"your mother has been in the state's prison for FORGERY!" My readers, you who have become parents, how does this impress your minds? Who among you does not feel for me and for them? What an uncle! What a cruel brother! What an inconsiderate father! For his children must sooner or later have a cast upon them that their father put his sister, their aunt, in prison for forgery. Who among you would purchase property at so dear a rate? During this life it can never be paid—the world cannot compensate me for what I have undergone. While in confinement, I had the pleasure of receiving a visit from the Rev. Dr. Peters,[61] who had lately come from London; he knew me from my infancy, and asked me what was the cause of my confinement; when I told him, he was surprised, saying that my father informed him that he had given his daughter a deed of two thousand acres of land. You will read his letter to me after my liberation—the contents are as follows:

> "The Rev. Harry Munro said in London, in 1778, that he had given to his daughter, Elizabeth Fisher, his patent right of two thousand acres of land in the county of Albany, eastward of Saratoga, that being all in his power to give her, and he feared it would be confiscated, because she and her husband were royalists; but as to his son, he said he had a rich mother, and the Jay family would take care that he should want for nothing."*

This has been a dear gift to me; I never wish to receive any more such.

I am told my father left a will, but I have not seen it; one copy was sent to my brother, the other to Montreal while I was in prison, so that it fell into the hands of my children; and ever since that time I was deprived of seeing them—they seem to act towards me with great coolness.—But why? Because I have been unfortunate and become poor. I shall now leave

---

*See also the Rev. Samuel Peters' letter stating this fact to Dr. Graham[62] and Sir James Jay.[63]

them to God and the world. From this day I will deny all family connextion. A hard sentence from a parent; but who, my candid reader, I again appeal to you, who, treated as I have been, would not do the same? Ten long years in a state of affliction and misery, and not so much as one of them to enquire [inquire] after their mother, or even to send a letter to me; and having been at liberty these four years, not a word have I received from them, till last summer my youngest son came to New-York to see my brother, on some business, and called on me, not as a mother, but as a stranger. He told me his brother Harry was a man of fortune—had married his second wife, and was father of five children. My readers may see by this that their ingratitude did not proceed from want, but from disposition. I think hard of my brother's conduct; but it is not to be compared with that of my children. Only reflect on them—for you that are become parents must acknowledge that I have a cause to disown them forever. My best wishes are for their welfare, and have not the least doubt but sooner or later they will become sensible to how much they have neglected me. Let me be what I may, still I am their mother. Can children, let them be ever so kind, repay their mother for what she has to undergo in body and in mind, in bringing them up till they are able to do for themselves? I say they cannot. But I found a friend when I was in distress, which was the Lord; he did more for me than all of them with all their money—he protected me through all my trials—he gave me health and strength to withstand my enemies—he raised up friends for me every where, in prison and out of prison. I must relate to my readers some incidents that took place while I was in prison. I had been there but three days when a distinction was made between me and the other prisoners—I wanted for nothing but liberty. There was a man, one of the keepers, and a widower, who was very fond of me, and nothing was wanting on his part to make my confinement agreeable. After I was at liberty, he was my friend, and I shall always acknowledge it; but his friendship turned to love. No man could love a woman more than he did me; but I must confess I did not love him with that sincere affection which would induce me to become his wife; many thought me ungrateful in this respect, but I am sure I was not; for how could that man live happy with me when I did not love him. I am in duty bound to say that he was sincere friend.

When I was a discharged from prison, though a stranger, I never was refused credit. I always mentioned that I had been lately discharged from the state's prison, and my creditors have never troubled me. I enjoy good health, a flow of spirits, and a calm mind—no way disturbed concerning the things of this world, I endeavour to live decent, and to do as I wish to be done by. Instead of my brother doing harm by sending me to prison, it has been the will of God to order it for my good. I can say with truth, that my heart is weaned from the cares of this world—every soul has my best wishes for its welfare. What a change! I never can be thankful enough for this happy change; for now, whether I have plenty or not to supply my wants, I am easy, for I know God is my friend, and he will, I trust, by my honest endeavours, supply my wants in this life. My sincere wish is that God may be pleased to work such a reformation in the hearts of my brother and my children. I do not wish them to go to the state's prison to obtain this reformation; but I wish this may take place in their hearts, and then they will feel as happy as I do. Although I am in the state of poverty, I am happy. I think I can say without vanity, that I possess a generous heart, and honorable in all my dealings. I am always happy to have it in my power to serve my fellow-creatures, without interested motives. If in my power to accomplish it, no person should be in want of the real comforts of life—all should be happy in this world.

In a future edition of this work, I shall endeavor to show by letters and affidavits, and leave the public to decide, how far I am guilty or innocent in this unnatural and unhappy circumstance which has taken place between my brother and myself; but for want of _____ [unclear] and money I must now conclude.

NOTES

1. *Harry Munro*—Rev. Henry (Harry) Munro (1730–1801) was born in Dingwell, Scotland. He first attended the University of St. Andrews, and later studied divinity at the University of Edinburgh. In 1757 he was ordained by the Church of Scotland and purchased an army chaplaincy. He most probably arrived in the colonies in 1757 with his regiment, the 77th Highland Regiment of Foot, and served with them on the mainland and later in the West Indies. In 1762, he left the regiment, received 2,000 acres of bounty land in Charlotte Township (later Washington County), N.Y., and moved to New York.

The name of Munro's first wife, Elizabeth's mother (b. ?–1759) and the widow of one of his fellow officers, remains unknown, as does the exact date of the marriage (it probably took place sometime between 1757 and 1759). In 1763, he married a Miss Stockton of Princeton, N.J.; she died a year later after giving birth to a son, who died in infancy. During this period Munro decided to join the Church of England; he was ordained in London in 1765. Upon returning to America, he was appointed by the Society for the Propagation of the Gospel in Foreign Parts as missionary at Phillipsburg (now Yonkers), N.Y. On March 21st, 1766, he remarried once again, to Eve Jay. In 1768 he moved to Albany, where he served as the last rector under the English crown at St. Peter's Church. From this time until the outbreak of the Revolution, he was actively preaching in the frontier settlements and the Indian tribes in the area, particularly the Mohawks. Known for his loyalist sympathies, he was imprisoned in late 1776. In October 1777, he escaped and joined the British forces in Canada, serving as an army chaplain. He left for England in 1778 and lived in Scotland from 1783 until his death in Edinburgh, on May 30, 1801 (*Dictionary of American Biography*, henceforth referred to as DAB).

2. *77th regiment of foot*—The Seventy-Seventh Highland Regiment of Foot (also known as Montgomery's Highlanders) commanded by Gen. Archibald Montgomery, was raised in Scotland in 1757. It arrived in the American colonies in 1758 and fought in Canada, New York, western Pennsylvania, South Carolina, and later in the Caribbean Islands. The regiment was disbanded in 1763, at which point the officers and men were offered land in the American colonies or passage back to Scotland. Elizabeth Fisher's father, Harry Munro, received 2,000 acres of bounty land near Hebron, N.Y. (DAB). *http://www.electricscotland.com/history/scotreg/montgomery.htm* (site visited Sept. 30, 2002).

3. *General Montgomery*—Archibald Montgomery (1726–1796), eleventh earl of Eglington, was a young major in the 36th Regiment of Foot at the outbreak of the Seven Years War. He soon raised his own regiment in Scotland and was appointed lieutenant colonel in 1757. After the end of the war and the disbandment of his regiment, he went on to a very successful military career (*Dictionary of National Biography*, henceforth referred to as DNB).

4. *Burlington*—Burlington (now Burlington City, N.J.) was founded by Quakers in 1677.

5. *Doctor Auchmuty*—Rev. Doc. Samuel Auchmuty (1722–1777), was the rector of Trinity Church at the time. He was a graduate of Harvard, and was ordained by the Church of England in 1747. A year later he became assistant minister of Trinity Church, and in 1764 became rector. During the Revolution, he strongly supported the loyalist cause. He died on March 4, 1777 (DAB).

6. *Trinity Church, New York City*—Trinity Church was established in 1697, and initially served the English Anglican population of New York. By the 1720s the majority of the Huguenot families in New York City, including the Jays, had joined Trinity Church. Peter Jay, Eve and John Jay's father, served there as vestryman for many years (Goodfriend 1991, 19; Morris 1975, 30, 33).

7. *Widow Chambers*—Ann Van Cortlandt Chambers (?—1774) was Eve Jay Munro's maternal aunt. She was the widow of John Chambers (1710–1765), one of the lawyers involved in the Zenger case (Morris 1975, 33).

8. *Miss Jay*—Eve Jay Munro (1728–1810) was the eldest daughter of Peter Jay and Mary Anna Van Courtland Jay and sister of John Jay. She evidently suffered

from fits, which her father termed "hystericks," from childhood well into her twenties (Morris 1975, 35). She was thirty-eight at the time of her marriage to Harry Munro, who clearly saw the social advantages of this marriage and intended to capitalize upon them. By Elizabeth Fisher's account it was an unhappy marriage, and indeed with the outbreak of the Revolution, Eve Jay Munro chose to remain with her son and her natal family. According to one source, she returned in 1779 to Albany to prevent her husband's name from being entered into an act of attainder (which would have entailed the loss of his property). She died in 1810 and is buried in Rye, N.Y. *http://www.nysm.nysed.gov/albany/bios/j/ejay1065.html* (site visited Sept. 30, 2002).

9. *Peter Jay*—Peter Jay (1704–1782), father of Eve Jay Munro and John Jay, was the son of Augustus and Anna Bayard Jay. He was a successful merchant and vestryman at Trinity Church in New York City. In 1745, after the birth of John Jay, the family moved to their farm near Rye, on Long Island Sound (Morris 1975, 30, 33).

10. *Philips' Manor*—The land on which Phillipsburg (now Yonkers), N.Y., was built first belonged to Dutch settlers. In 1672 ownership of the settlement passed to the Philipse family. Harry Munro was appointed there (in 1765) as a missionary by the Society for the Propagation of the Gospel in Foreign Parts.

11. *Rye*—Rye is located east of Mamaroneck, on Long Island Sound (some 32 miles north of New York City). The Jay family farm, which remained in the family until 1904, was located there.

12. *Peter Jay Munro*—Peter Jay Munro (1767–1833) was educated since childhood by his maternal uncle, John Jay. At the age of thirteen (1779), Munro accompanied John Jay to his diplomatic posting in Spain, and later to France (1782), where he served as his uncle's official secretary. Upon returning to New York in 1784, he began his legal studies, interning at the office of Aaron Burr. He was admitted to the bar and elected to public office; until 1826 (when he was paralyzed by a stroke and retired) he was considered one of the leading lawyers of New York. He died on Sept. 23, 1833. *http://www.famousamericans.net/henrymunro/* (site visited Sept. 30, 2002).

13. *William Reid*—A William Reid, who arrived in America from Scotland in 1764, is known to have lived in the Salem area at the time. Later, suspected of having loyalist sympathies, he was imprisoned by the patriots (Mahaffy 1999).

14. *Duncan Campbell*—Duncan Campbell was the father of Alexander and James Campbell of Schenectady, N.Y. Schenectady was a prosperous trading community. The main trade road from the west to Albany passed through the town and the Mohawk River became navigable from that point. The family supported the loyalist cause and left for Canada during the war. (For more details see the following entry and note 34).

15. *Alexander Campbell*—An Alexander Campbell (1734–1800), a loyalist, formerly of Schenectady, N.Y, is known to have lived in Montreal after the Revolution. His date of birth would make him about forty years of age at the time of the proposed marriage, and he may indeed be the eldest son of Duncan Campbell of Schenectady, N.Y. Although the marriage never took place, the two families must have maintained some contact, for Alexander Campbell and his brother James later signed a document (at Elizabeth Munro Fisher's request) testifying to Henry Munro's title to the 2,000 acres of land near Hebron, N.Y. *http://www.usinternet.com/users/dfnels/goddard.htm* (site visited Sept. 30, 2002).

16. *Governor Colden*—Cadwallader Colden (1688–1776) was born in Ireland to Scottish parents. After studying medicine in London, he arrived in Philadelphia (1710), and later moved to New York (1718). Two years later he was appointed surveyor general, and in 1721 was appointed to the governor's council. Over the next forty years he became one of the more influential men in New York and in 1761 was appointed lieutenant governor of the colony, serving intermittently as acting governor and lieutenant governor until 1775. During the growing unrest in the 1760s Colden became increasingly unpopular through a series of political and legal decisions, which alienated many colonists and has led to one historian naming him "the unwitting provocateur of the early revolutionary movement in New York (Kammen 1987, 346). Colden was also one of the most learned men in the colonies, corresponding and writing extensively on mathematics, botany, physics, medicine, and philosophy. In 1751, he published *The Principles of Action in Matter*, his revised critique of Newton's work. He also wrote *The History of the Five Indian Nations* (1727) on the Iroquois tribes (DAB).

Fisher confused Colden (who did not commit suicide) with one of his predecessors, Governor Osborne (who did). She corrects herself later in the paragraph.

17. *Governor Osborn*—Sir Danvers Osborne (?–1753) was appointed governor of New York in 1753. A few days after his arrival he committed suicide by hanging himself with his tie in the garden of lodgings (Kammen 1987, 301). A letter from Peter Jay, dated Oct. 24, 1753, described the incident (Morris 1975, 37); another item relating the event is a letter of condolence written by Lt. Governor Delancy to the Lords of Trade, the letter can be found at: *http://www.geocities.com/christman19/mvfk03.html* (site visited Aug. 2, 2002).

18. *Mr. Fisher*—Donald Fisher (?–1799), Elizabeth Munro Fisher's husband, was born in Killin, Perthshire, Scotland. According to Fisher, he served in the 77th Regiment of Foot before their marriage on Feb. 2, 1776. He served with Burgoyne and after Saratoga left for Canada. According to one source, in 1786 Donald Fisher claimed 2,200 acres with improvements by Alexander and Finlay Fisher and Malcolm McNaughton, near Granville Township (Salem, N.Y.). It is possible that Donald Fisher himself had received this land as bounty in lieu of his services or that he was claiming his father-in-law's land. Donald and Elizabeth had five

children, only the names of their eldest son (Henry Munro Fisher) and one daughter (Eliza Fisher) are known. He died in Montreal in February 1799. *http://www.televar.com/~gmorin/fisher.htm* (site visited Sept. 30, 2002).

19. *Governor Tryon*—William Tryon (1729–1788) was appointed lieutenant governor of North Carolina in 1764, and a year later became governor. During this tenure in office he gained notoriety by violently suppressing the Regulator movement in the colony. He served in North Carolina until 1771, when he was appointed governor of New York. He remained in New York until the outbreak of the Revolution (DNB).

20. *Mr. Vesterlowe*—Eilardus Westerlo (1737–1790) was born in Groningen, Holland. After graduating from the University of Groningen (1760), he immigrated to America and became pastor of the Albany Dutch Reformed Church (where Elizabeth Munro and Donald Fisher were married). In 1775 he made an advantageous marriage to Catherine Livingston, widow of Stephen Van Renssalaer II. Westerlo supported the patriot cause during the Revolution (DAB).

21. *Birth of her son*—Elizabeth Fisher's eldest son, *Henry Munro Fisher* was born on November 14, 1776, in Hebron, N.Y. Very little is known about his early life. He probably moved with the family to Montreal in 1777, Elizabeth Fisher mentioned later in the *Memoirs* that she apprenticed him to Isaac Todd, a Montreal trader, heavily involved in the fur-trade. He was first married to Madeleine Gauthier de Verville (ca. 1796), and later married his second wife Marie Ann La Saliere (ca. 1810). He died on May 21, 1846 in Prairie du Chien, Wisconsin. *http://ww.televar.com/~gmorin/fisher.htm* (site visited Sept. 30, 2002).

22. *Broken breast*—An all-encompassing term for breast abscesses women developed during nursing. Extremely painful, they were treated with poultices and as a last resort, lanced and drained (see Ulrich 1990, 196–97).

23. *General Burgoyne*—John Burgoyne (1722–1792) returned to America in 1777 to command the army entering New York from Canada. He was defeated at Saratoga by the American forces under the command of Horatio Gates; Burgoyne and his army were taken prisoner. Released on parole in 1778, he returned to England, took up his seat in Parliament, and opposed the war (DNB).

24. *Skeennsborough*—Skenesborough (now Whitehall, N.Y.) lies just south of the southern end of Lake Champlain. At the time the town had a sawmill and boatyard owned by Maj. Phillip Skene; several of the vessels that later took part in the battle of Valcour Island, were built there (Blanco 1993, 1683–89).

25. *Colonel Williams*—John Williams (1752–1806) was born in Barnstable, England. He studied medicine in St. Thomas Hospital in London and served for one year as a surgeon's mate in the navy before immigrating to America in 1773. Williams settled in Salem, Washington Co., N.Y., and was elected to the State Provincial Congress in 1775. He was appointed in the militia as colonel of the

Washington County Regiment in 1776 and commanded it throughout the war. He held several public and political posts and was elected as a Federalist to the Fourth and Fifth Congresses (1795–1799). He died in Salem, N.Y., on July 22, 1806 (DAB).

26. *John Baker*—John Baker (?—1830) from Saratoga County was registered as a militiaman from Albany County, serving in the 8th Regiment (Roberts and Mather 1996: 111); see also *http://freepages.genealogy.rootsweb.com/~terrybigler/ descendantsofsimonbaker.htm* (site visited Oct. 18, 2002).

27. *Death of General Frazer*—Simon Fraser (1729–1777) was born in Scotland. He first entered the Dutch service in 1748, beginning his career in the British army in 1755. He took part during the Seven Years War in the sieges of Louisbourg, Cape Breton Island (1758), and Quebec (1759). During the Revolutionary War, he was deployed with the 24th Regiment of Foot to Canada. Fraser commanded the British forces at Trois Rivières (1776), after which he was granted the commission of brigadier general. Later in the war as commander of Burgoyne's Advanced Corps, he took part in the capture of Fort Ticonderoga and the battle of Hubbardton. Fraser commanded the right flank of the British forces during the First Battle of Saratoga (Sept. 19, 1777) and did so again during the second. He was mortally wounded during the Second Battle of Saratoga (Oct. 7, 1777), reputedly by Private Timothy Murphy of Morgan's Riflemen, as he rode among his troops encouraging them to stand and cover the retreating British forces. He, along with other wounded officers, was brought to Taylor House, Baroness Fredreika von Riedesel's quarters. He died there early the next morning and was buried in the battlefield (Blanco 1993, 594–98).

28. *Saratoga*—Fisher is referring to the First Battle of Saratoga (also known as the Battle of Stillwater or the Battle of Freeman's Farm), which took place on Sept. 19, 1777, near the town of Stillwater, N.Y. The American forces lost the battle on that day (Blanco 1993).

29. *Battle of Saratoga*—Fisher is actually referring to the Second Battle of Saratoga (also referred to as the Battle of Bemis Heights), which took place on Oct. 7, 1777. The Battle of Saratoga is considered a major turning point of the American Revolution. In the campaign of 1777, Burgoyne planned a three-pronged advance on Albany. He led the main column, moving southward along the Hudson River. Initially the plan seemed to be working; Burgoyne's forces were constantly pushing the Americans southward, suffering only minor casualties. This advance was halted at Saratoga. Gen. Horatio Gates, the new commander of the Northern Department, led the American forces at both battles of Saratoga. Burgoyne and his army surrendered to Gates on Oct. 17, 1777 (Blanco 1993).

30. *Diamond Island*—Diamond Island lies in Lake George, N.Y. Gen. Burgoyne fortified the island after he captured Fort Ticonderoga and Mt. Independence.

31. *Monat Independent*—Fisher was most likely referring to Mount Independence, Vermont. It is a high, rocky promontory jutting north into Lake Champlain, directly opposite Fort Ticonderoga. Protected by water and steep cliffs on three sides, it is accessible by land only from the south.

32. *General Powell*—Brig.-Gen. Henry Watson Powell (?–?) was in command of Burgoyne's 2nd Brigade from May 1777. In August 1777, he commanded Fort Ticonderoga. *http://www.revwar75.com/crown/brigade.htm* (site visited Oct. 2, 2002).

33. *William Aird, Montreal*—Possibly related to James Aird (?—1819), a Scottish fur trader who traded in the Great Lakes area, by 1786 he was based in Prairie du Chien. Taking into account, the Fishers' future association with the fur trade in general, and Prairie du Chien in particular, the connection is more than likely.

34. *James Campbell*—Son of Duncan Campbell of Schenectady, N.Y., and younger brother of Alexander Campbell. There are several James Campbells listed in Quebec in this period; it is unclear which of them is the one mentioned here (*Dictionary of Canadian Biography*, henceforth referred to as DCB).

35. *Alexander Fisher*—Alexander Fisher was Donald Fisher's cousin. He too sided with the loyalists during the Revolution and came to Montreal after the Battle of Saratoga (DCB).

36. *Judge Frazer, Montreal*—Malcolm Fraser (1733–1815), was a wealthy landowner from Quebec. He was first appointed justice of the peace in 1764, a post he held for several years (DCB).

37. *Col. Jessup*—Edward Jessup (1735–1816) was born in Stamford, Conn.; during his childhood the family moved to the Albany area. Jessup fought with the Provincial Corps against the French during the Seven Years War. After the war Jessup and his brothers emerged as prominent businessmen in Albany and owned land on the upper Hudson River. Jessup himself was appointed justice of the peace in Albany. During the Revolution the Jessups took up the loyalist cause, raised a Corps of Loyalists (Jessup's Corps) and fought with Burgoyne in the 1777 campaign. After the surrender at Saratoga, the Corps was restructured and renamed the Loyal Rangers (Jessup's Rangers). When the Revolutionary War ended Jessup and his men received land grants in Canada, around the Kingston area on the northern shore of the St. Lawrence River (DCB).

38. *Isaac Todd*—Isaac Todd (1742–1819) was born in Ireland. He came to Canada around 1760 and by 1765 he had established himself as a merchant in Montreal. Todd's trading activities ranged all around the Great Lakes area, and his firm imported from London a wide variety of European trade goods. As a leader of the city's fur-trade community he often represented the fur traders' interests in England. Todd was often involved in political activities and public life and was commissioned justice of the peace since 1765 (DCB).

39. *Caldwell Manor*—During the early French period the area around the present day town of St. Georges de Clarenceville, Quebec, was known as the Seigneuirie de Foucault. In 1774, the area was leased to Col. Henry Caldwell and came to be known as Caldwell's Manor. It lies midway between the Richelieu River (on the west) and Missisquoi Bay (on the east).

40. *Joseph Mott*—Joseph Mott, son of Joseph and Deborah Mott, was born in Hempstead (Long Island), N.Y. The family had loyalist sympathies and Mott, his son, and some other relatives moved to northwestern Vermont sometime between 1789 and Elizabeth Fisher's visit in 1790. *http://webpages.charter.net/treinhardt/surnames/mott/mott.html* (site visited Oct. 2, 2002).

41. *Mr. Duer*—Fisher is most likely referring to Judge William Duer (1747–?), who purchased a large tract of land (including river falls) on the Hudson River in 1768 near Fort Edward, N.Y. He soon built a sawmill and a gristmill, was active in public affairs and held numerous public offices. *http://www.fortedwardnewyork.net. history.htm* (site visited Oct. 1, 2002).

42. *Mr. Fisher's nephew*—Elizabeth Fisher was most likely referring to Finlay Fisher (c. 1756–1819) or his brother, Alexander. Both had emigrated from Scotland to Charlotte (Washington) County, N.Y. and began farming. Both Finlay Fisher and his brother Alexander were mentioned later in Donald Fisher's land claim. Like many other loyalists in the area they joined Burgoyne's forces; after Saratoga they came to Montreal, as did their cousins Duncan, James, John, and Alexander Fisher (DCB). *http://www.televar.com/~gmorin/fisher.htm* (site visited Sept. 30, 2002).

43. *Wind-Mill Point*—There are three locations on Lake Champlain that were referred to as Windmill Point. The first, which bears the name to the present day, is situated on the lake near Alburgh, Vermont. The place takes its name from a large stone windmill built by the French settlers. It was here that Benedict Arnold anchored his fleet before the battle of Valcour Island (Oct. 11, 1776). The second location referred to by this name lies south of Crown Point, and the third is Colchester Point.

44. *Isle of Noah*—Fisher was probably referring to the Ile aux Noix, a small island, which lies in the Richelieu River, Quebec.

45. *1785*—Fisher was mistaken about the date of her visit. She in fact visited the Jays in November 1784. (Letter from Peter Jay Munro to John Jay, dated November 24, 1784). *http://www.columbia.edu/cu/lweb/eresources/arcives.jay/* (site visited April 15, 2003).

46. *John Jay*—John Jay (1745–1829), son of Peter Jay and Mary Anna Van Courtland Jay, was born on December 12, 1745, in New York City. He was educated at King's (Columbia) College, and was admitted to the bar in 1768. Originally, he was not enthusiastic in his support for the Revolution in both Continental Congresses. Only after the Declaration of Independence was issued did he

become active in the work of the Provincial Congress. As a member of the Constitutional Convention, he helped draft the final version of the 1777 Constitution, and soon after was elected the first Chief Justice of the Supreme Court of New York. Jay served as president of the Continental Congress between 1778 and 1779, when he left on a diplomatic mission to Spain. In 1782 he joined the American Peace Commission in Paris. After his return home, Jay was appointed Secretary for Foreign Affairs in late 1784. He served in that capacity until the fall of 1789 when he was appointed the first Chief Justice of the United States. Jay also served as minister to Britain (while still Chief Justice), negotiating the controversial 1794 treaty that bears his name. He returned to the United States in 1795, resigned his post as Chief Justice, and was twice elected to the governorship of New York. He retired from public office in 1801, and died on his country estate near Bedford, N.Y., on May 14, 1829 (DAB).

47. *John Strong Esq.*—Fisher was probably referring to John Strang (1751–1829) of Yorktown, N.Y., who in the 1770s was John Jay's law clerk (Morris 1975, 145), and by now had set up his own practice. A John Strang Esq. appears in the 1790 Federal Census of Westchester Co., N.Y. *http://www.rootsweb.com/ ~nywestch/census/york1790.htm* (site visited April 15, 2003).

48. *Harry Munro's letter to Elizabeth Fisher*—Harry Munro seems to have pitted his children against each other. It is clear from his later correspondence that he retained his ties to his son Peter Jay Munro, corresponded rather cordially with John Jay, and was visited in Edinburgh by John Jay's son, to whom he entrusted some of his papers (letter from Harry Munro to John Jay, dated December 24, 1794).

During Elizabeth Fisher's visit, Peter Jay Munro sent a letter to John Jay remarking, "[M]y father's conduct to me was blamable, but towards her it has been scandalous to the last Degree . . ." (letter dated November 24, 1784). It is possible that Harry Munro instructed Elizabeth to discontinue her visits to the Jays for fear his two children might find out that he promised each of them to leave his property only to them. Most of the Jay family papers are available online at: *http://www. columbia.edu/cu/lweb/eresources/arcives.jay/* (site visited April 15, 2003).

49. *Slut*—bitch, (archaic) a female dog.

50. *Carman*—a person who drives, or conveys goods by car.

51. *Capt. Grant, Montreal*—Alexander Grant (1734–1813) was born in Glenmoriston, Scotland. He served in the Royal Navy between 1755 and 1757; he then joined the 77th Highland Regiment (Harry Munro's regiment). For most of the Seven Years War, Grant served on various vessels on Lake Champlain and the Hudson River. After the war, Grant became naval superintendent and moved to Detroit (1774). Grant realized this opportunity and soon began building his own fleet of vessels and establishing his position as one of the leading merchants in the area. During the Revolutionary War, Grant commanded the British naval forces on the Great Lakes.

The war reversed Grant's fortunes; he was forced to sell his ships and lost some 12,000 acres of land in New York. In 1786, Grant was first appointed justice of the peace in western Quebec (a post to which he was reappointed continuously until his death in 1813). In the course of the following years, he held several other civic and political posts; most notable was the position of the administrator of Upper Canada (1805–1806). In 1812 Grant retired to his family farm near Grosse Point, Mich., where he died the following year (DCB).

52. *Cumberton Head*—Fisher was probably referring to Cumberland Head, N.Y. on Lake Champlain.

53. *St. John's*—St. Johns, Quebec, was one of the British bases on the Richelieu River, just above Lake Champlain.

54. *Samuel Young*—Fisher was most likely referring to Samuel Young (1779–1850) of Saratoga Co., N.Y. At the time Young was probably studying law at the firm of Levi H. Palmer in Ballston, N.Y.; by 1813 Young was serving as justice of the peace. *www.rootsweb.com/~nysarato/Sylvester/chap27.html* (site visited Apr. 15 2003).

55. *Quit claim*—A quitclaim deed is a legal instrument used to release one person's right, title, or interest to another without providing a guarantee or warranty of title.

56. *Rupert*—Fisher was referring to the town of Rupert, Vermont, which is located in the northwestern part of Bennington Co., some twenty-six miles north of the town of Bennington.

57. *Adonijah Crane*—Two men, Addanijah Crain and Addanijah Crain Jr., are listed in the 1790 census of the township of Rupert, Vermont. *www.rootsweb. com/~vtgenweb/vtbennin/1790RupertVT.html* (site visited Apr. 15, 2003).

58. *Thomas Eddy*—Thomas Eddy (1758–1827) was born in Philadelphia, to a Quaker family with loyalist sympathies. He eventually settled in New York City and became a successful insurance broker and underwriter. Increasingly he began to devote himself to philanthropic work, particularly prison reform. Eddy and some associates (including John Murray) convinced the New York legislature to construct more modern prisons (which would incorporate a single-cell system). Eventually only one prison was built, "Newgate Prison" in Greenwich Village (where Elizabeth Munro Fisher was imprisoned from 1800 to 1806). Besides prison reform, Eddy was involved in several other social reform movements and projects. (DAB)

59. *John Murray*—John Murray (1737–1808) was born near Lancaster, Pa., to a Quaker family. In 1753, Murray and his brother Robert moved to New York City, established an import business and eventually became one of the leading shipowners in the colonies. During the Revolution the Murrays, like many other Quakers, attempted to maintain some form of neutrality. This position did not affect his economic position; when the war ended he became a member of the Chamber of Commerce (1787–1806) and later was elected a director of the Bank of New York.

Murray had a strong commitment to philanthropic work in the city. He was a member of the commission (which included Thomas Eddy) appointed to build the new state prison and helped establish education programs for poor children. Together with Eddy, he was involved in several efforts to improve the conditions of the Oneidas and other Indian tribes in New York (DAB).

60. *Governor Lewis*—Lewis Morgan (1754–1844) served at the time as governor of New York (1804–1807). Before holding this post he had served as the state's attorney general and Chief Justice of the New York Supreme Court (DAB).

61. *Rev. Dr. Peters, London*—Samuel Andrew Peters (1735–1826), was born in Hebron, Conn. He studied at Yale and later at King's College. In 1758, he traveled to England and was ordained by the Church of England; a year later he was appointed missionary by the Society for the Propagation of the Gospel in Foreign Parts. In 1760, he returned to America and served as rector of the Anglican Church in Hebron until 1774. He openly came out in favor of the loyalist cause and as a result was harassed several times by the Sons of Liberty during the summer and fall of 1774, until eventually he left for England. He lived in London from 1774 till 1794, often writing for periodicals. He was elected bishop of Vermont in 1794, but as the Church of England could no longer create American bishops, he was never consecrated. In 1805, he returned to America in order to further the claims of the American heirs of the explorer Jonathan Carver (1710–1780) to a large tract of land near St. Anthony's Falls (present day Minneapolis). In late 1806, Peters eventually bought the claim from Carver's heirs and succeeded in interesting a group of New York merchants in a scheme to settle the land. It was probably during one of these visits that he met with Elizabeth Fisher. In 1826, the year of his death, Congress invalidated the claim (DAB).

62. *Dr. Graham*—Fisher was most likely confusing Dr. Andrew Graham (1728–1785) of Southbury, Conn., (who was deceased at the time) with his son John Andrew Graham. John Andrew Graham (1764–1841) was one of the leading and most eloquent criminal attorneys in New York. Between 1785 and 1803 the younger Graham had been a resident of Rutland, Vt., and admitted to the bar of the state's supreme court. Both Grahams were close friends of Rev. Peters (DAB).

63. *Sir James Jay*—James Jay (1732–1815) was Peter Jay and Mary Anna Van Courtland Jay's third son and John Jay's older brother. James Jay studied medicine at the University of Edinburgh and returned to practice in New York; he was knighted in 1763. He initially supported the revolutionary cause and was a member of the New York senate (1778–1782). In 1782 he went over to the British. This sudden change of sides caused a permanent rift between James and John Jay. James Jay eventually returned to the United States and died in Springfield, N.Y., in 1815 (DAB).

Bibliography

Alby, Eliza Ann Dow. 1840?. *Life and Adventures of Eliza Ann Dow.* n.p., n.d.

Allen, Graham. 2000. *Intertextuality.* London and New York: Routledge.

Arch, Stephen Carl. 2001. *After Franklin: The Emergence of Autobiography in Post-Revolutionary America, 1780–1830.* Hanover and London: University of New Hampshire Press.

Arkow, Phil. 1996. The relationship between animal abuse and other forms of family violence. *Family Violence and Sexual Assault Bulletin* 12: 29–34.

Armstrong, Nancy. 1998. Captivity and cultural capital in the English novel. *Novel* 31: 373–98.

Aronson, Amy Beth. 2002. *Taking Liberties: Early American Women's Magazines and Their Readers.* Westport, Conn.: Praeger.

Bailyn, Bernard. 1986. *Voyagers to the West: A Passage in the Peopling of America.* New York: Knopf.

Barnes, Elizabeth. 1997. *States of Sympathies: Seduction and Democracy in the American Novel.* New York: Columbia University Press.

Baym, Nina. 1984. *Novels, Readers, and Reviewers: Responses to Fiction in Antebellum America.* Ithaca: Cornell University Press.

Benstock, Shari. 1998. Authorizing the autobiographical. In Smith and Watson, 145–55.

Blanco, Richard L., ed. 1993. *The American Revolution, 1775–1783: An Encyclopedia.* 2 vols. New York and London: Garland.

Bloch, Ruth H. 1987. The gendered meanings of virtue in revolutionary America. *Signs* 13: 37–58.

———. American feminine ideals in transition: The rise of the Moral Mother, 1785–1815.*Feminist Studies* 4: 101–26.

Boudreau, Kristin. 1997. Early American criminal narratives and the problem of public sentiments. *Early American Literature* 32: 249–69.

Boureau, Alain. 2001. *The Myth of Pope Joan.* Translated by Lydia G. Cochrane. Chicago and London: University of Chicago Press.

Branson, Susan. 1996. Beyond respectability: The female world of love and crime. *Studies in Eighteenth-Century Culture* 25: 245–64.

Castiglia, Christopher. 1996. *Bound and Determined: Captivity, Culture-Crossing, and White Womanhood from Mary Rowlandson to Patty Hearst.* Chicago: University of Chicago Press.

Cohen, Daniel A., ed. 1997. *The Female Marine and Related Works: Narratives of Cross-Dressing and Urban Vice in America's Early Republic.* Amherst: University of Massachusetts Press.

Cohen, Patricia Cline. 1999. *The Murder of Helen Jewett: The Life and Death of a Prostitute in Nineteenth-Century New York.* New York: Vintage Books.

Cott, Nancy F. 1977. *The Bonds of Womanhood: "Woman's Sphere" in New England, 1780–1835.* New Haven: Yale University Press.

Cressy, David. 1996. Gender trouble and cross-dressing in early modern England. *Journal of British Studies* 35: 438–65.

Darnton, Robert. 1984. Workers revolt: The Great Cat Massacre of the Rue Saint-Sévérein. In *The Great Cat Massacre and Other Episodes in French Cultural History,* 75–106. New York: Basic Books.

Davidoff, Leonore, and Catherine Hall. 1987. *Family Fortunes: Men and Women of the English Middle Class, 1780–1850.* Chicago: University of Chicago Press.

Davidson, Cathy N. 1998. No more separate spheres! *American Literature* 70: 443–63.

———. 1993. The novel as subversive activity: Women reading, women writing. In *Beyond the American Revolution: Explorations in the History of American Radicalism,* ed. Alfred F. Young, 283–316. DeKalb: Northern Illinois University Press.

De Grave, Kathleen. 1995. *Swindler, Spy, and Rebel: The Confidence Woman in Nineteenth-Century America.* Columbia and London: University of Missouri Press.

Dekker, Rodolf M., and Lotte C. Van der Pol. 1989. Republican heroines and cross-dressing women in the French revolutionary armies. *History of European Ideas* 10: 353–64.

Dolan, Frances E. 1994. *Dangerous Familiars: Representations of Domestic Crime in England, 1550–1700*. Ithaca: Cornell University Press.

Dugaw, Dianne. 1989. *Warrior Women and Popular Balladry, 1650–1850*. Cambridge: Cambridge University Press.

————. 1986. Structural analysis of the female warrior ballad: The landscape of a world turned upside down. *Journal of Folklore Research* 23: 23–42.

Dictionary of American Biography. 1958–1964. New York: Scribners.

Dictionary of Canadian Biography. 1983. Toronto, Buffalo, and London: University of Toronto Press.

Ebersole, Gary L. 1995. *Captured By Texts: Puritan to Post Modern Images of Indian Captivity*. Charlottesville and London: University Press of Virginia.

Fahrner, Robert. 1993. A reassessment of Garrick's *The Male coquette; or Seventeen-Hundred and Fifty-Seven* as veiled discourse. *Eighteenth-Century Life* 17 (3): 1–13.

Favret, Mary A. 1994. Telling tales about genre: Poetry in the Romantic novel. *Studies in the Novel* 26: 153–72.

Flaum, Eric. 1993. *The Encyclopedia of Mythology: Gods, Heroes, and Legends of the Greeks and Romans*. Philadelphia: Courage Books.

Flynn, Clifton P. 1999. Exploring the link between corporal punishment and childhood animal cruelty. *Journal of Marriage and the Family* 61: 971–81.

Franklin, H. Bruce. 1989. *Prison Literature in America: The Victim as Criminal and Artist*. New York: Oxford University Press.

Frazier, Patrick. 1992. *The Mohicans of Stockbridge*. Lincoln: University of Nebraska Press.

Gagnier, Regenia. 1991. *Subjectivities: A History of Self-Representation in Britain, 1832–1920*. New York and Oxford: Oxford University Press.

Goodfriend, Joyce D. 1991. *Before the Melting Pot: Society and Culture in Colonial New York City, 1664–1730*. Princeton: Princeton University Press.

Gordon, Linda. 1988. *Heroes of Their Own Lives; The Politics and History of Family Violence, Boston 1880–1960*. London: Virago Press.

Gorn, Elliott J. 1985. "Gouge and bite, pull hair and scratch": The social significance of fighting in the southern backcountry. *American Historical Review* 90: 18–43.

Gowing, Laura. 1993. Gender and the language of insult in early modern London. *History Workshop Journal* 35: 1–21.

Greene, Jack P., and J. R. Pole, eds. 1991. *The Blackwell Encyclopedia of the American Revolution*. Oxford: Blackwell.

Halevi, Sharon. 1995. The path not taken: Class, gender, and race in the South Carolina backcountry, 1750–1800. Ph.D. diss., University of Iowa.

Hall, David D. 1996. The politics of writing and reading in eighteenth-century America. In *Cultures of Print: Essays in the History of the Book*. Amherst: University of Massachusetts Press.

Hall, Max. [1960] 1990. *Benjamin Franklin and Polly Baker: The History of a Literary Deception*. Pittsburgh: Pittsburgh University Press.

Hasan-Rokem, Galit, and Alan Dundes, eds. 1986. *The Wandering Jew: Essays in the Interpretation of a Christian Legend*. Bloomington: Indiana University Press.

Hessinger, Rodney. 1998. "Insidious murderers of female innocence": Representations of masculinity in the seduction tales of the late eighteenth century. In *Sex and Sexuality in Early America*, ed. Merril D. Smith, 262–82. New York: New York University Press.

Hill, Elizabeth Freeman. 1852. *The Widow's Offering*. New London: D. S. Ruddock.

Hiltner, Judith. 1999. "She bled in secret": Deborah Sampson, Herman Mann, and *The Female Review*. *Early American Literature* 34: 190–220.

Jelinek, Estelle C. 1987. Disguise autobiographies: Women masquerading as men. *Women's Studies International Forum* 10: 53–62.

Juster, Susan. 1991. "In a different voice": Male and female narratives of religious conversion in post-revolutionary America. *American Quarterly* 41: 34–62.

Kammen, Michael. 1987. *Colonial New York: A History*. White Plains, N.Y.: KTO Press.

Kane, Stuart A. 1996. Wives with knives: Early modern ballads and the transgressive commodity. *Criticism* 28: 219–37.

Keetley, Dawn. 1999. Victim and victimizer: Female fiends and unease over marriage in antebellum sensational fiction. *American Quarterly* 51: 344–84.

———. 1998. Beautiful poisoners: "Rappaccini's Daughter," Hannah Kinney's 1840 murder trial and the problem of criminal responsibility. *ESQ—A Journal of the American Renaissance* 44: 125–59.

Kelley, Mary. 2001. Beyond the boundaries. *Journal of the Early Republic* 21: 73–78.

———. 1984. *Private Woman, Public Stage: Literary Domesticity in Nineteenth-Century America*. New York: Oxford University Press.

Kerber, Linda K. 1989. "History can do it no justice:" Women and the reinterpretation of the American Revolution. In *Women in the Age of the American Revolution*, ed. Ronald Hoffman and Peter J. Albert, 3–42. Charlottesville: University of Virginia Press.

———. 1988. Separate spheres, female worlds, woman's place: The rhetoric of women's history. *Journal of American History* 75: 9–39.

———. [1980] 1986. *Women of the Republic: Intellect and Ideology in Revolutionary America.* New York and London: W. W. Norton.

Kim, Sung Bok. 1982. Impact of class relations and warfare in the American Revolution: The New York experience. *Journal of American History* 69: 326–46.

———. 1970. A new look at the great landlords of eighteenth-century New York.*William and Mary Quarterly*, 3rd ser., 28: 581–614.

Kritzer, Amelia Howe. 1996. Playing with Republican Motherhood: Self-representation in plays by Susanna Haswell Rowson and Judith Sargent Murray. *Early American Literature* 31: 150–66.

Lehuu, Isabelle. 2000. *Carnival on the Page: Popular Print Media in Antebellum America.* Chapel Hill and London: University of North Carolina Press.

Lerner, Gerda. 1969. The lady and the mill girl: Changes in the status of women in the age of Jackson. *Midcontinent American Studies Journal* 10: 5–15.

Lewis, Jan. 1987. The republican wife: Virtue and seduction in the early republic. *William and Mary Quarterly*, 3rd ser., 44: 689–721.

List, Karen K. 1994. Realities and possibilities: The lives of women in periodicals of the new republic. *American Journalism* 11: 20–38.

McCall. Laura. 2001. "Shall I fetter her will?": Literary Americans confront feminine submission, 1820–1860. *Journal of the Early Republic* 21: 95–113.

Miles, Lion G. 1994. The red man dispossessed: The Williams family and the alienation of Indian land in Stockbridge, Massachusetts, 1736–1818. *New England Quarterly* 67: 46–76.

Morris, Richard B., ed. 1972. *John Jay: The Making of a Revolutionary, 1745–1780: Unpublished Papers.* New York: Harper and Row.

Namias, June. 1993. *White Captives: Gender and Ethnicity on the American Frontier.* Chapel Hill: University of North Carolina Press.

Norton, Mary Beth. 1986. Gender and defamation in seventeenth-century Virginia. *William and Mary Quarterly*, 3rd ser., 44: 411–26.

———. 1976. Eighteenth-Century American women in peace and war: The case of the loyalists. *William and Mary Quarterly*, 3rd ser., 33: 386–409.

———. [1972] 1974. *The British-Americans: The Loyalist Exiles in England, 1774–1789.* London: Constable.

Nussbaum, Felicity A. 1989. *The Autobiographical Subject: Gender and Ideology in Eighteenth-Century England.* Baltimore and London: Johns Hopkins University Press.

Paradise, Nathaniel. 1995. Interpolated poetry, the novel, and female accomplishment. *Philological Quarterly* 74: 57–76.

Robb, George. 1997. Circe in crinoline: Domestic poisonings in Victorian England. *Journal of Family History* 22: 176–90.

Roberts, James A., and Frederic G. Mather, eds. 1996. *New York in the Revolution as a Colony and State.* Baltimore: Genealogical Publications Co. 2nd ed.

Samuels, Shirley. 1996. *Romances of the Republic: Women, the Family, and Violence in the Literature of the Early American Nation.* New York and Oxford: Oxford University Press.

———. 1986. The family, the state, and the novel in the early republic. *American Quarterly* 38: 381–395.

Scott, James C. 1990. *Domination and the Arts of Resistance: Hidden Transcripts.* New Haven and London: Yale University Press.

Sobel, Mechal. 2000. *Teach Me Dreams: The Search for Self in the Revolutionary Era.* Princeton and Oxford: Oxford University Press.

Shumsky, Neil Larry. 1976. Parents, children, and the selection of mates in colonial Virginia. *Eighteenth-Century Life* 2: 83–88.

Smith, Sidonie, and Julia Watson. 1998. Introduction: Situating subjectivity in women's autobiographical practices. In *Women, Autobiography, Theory: A Reader,* ed. Sidonie Smith and Julia Watson, 3–52. Madison: University of Wisconsin Press.

Smith-Rosenberg, Carroll. 1993. Captured subjects/ savage others: Violently engendering the new American. *Gender & History* 5: 177–95.

———. 1975. The female world of love and ritual: Relations between women in nineteenth-century America. *Signs* 1: 1–29.

Stephen, Leslie, and Sidney Lee, eds. 1964 [1917–]. *Dictionary of National Biography.* Oxford: Oxford University Press.

Stephens, Ellen. 1840. *The Cabin-boy Wife.* New York, C. E. Daniels.

Taves, Ann, ed. 1989. *Religion and Domestic Violence in Early New England: The Memoirs of Abigail Abbot Bailey.* Bloomington and Indianapolis: Indiana University Press.

Ulrich, Laurel Thatcher. 1990. *A Midwife's Tale: The Life of Martha Ballard, Based on Her Diary, 1785–1812.* New York: Vintage Books.

Wahrman, Dror. 1998. Percy's Prologue: From gender play to gender panic in eighteenth-century England. *Past and Present* 159: 113–60.

Welter, Barbara. 1966. The cult of true womanhood: 1820–1860. *American Quarterly* 18: 151–74.

Whyte, Martin King. 1992. Choosing mates—The American way. *Society* 29: 71–77.

Williams, Daniel E. 1986. "Behold a tragic scene strangely changed into a theater of mercy": The structure and significance of criminal conversion narratives in early New England. *American Quarterly* 38: 827–47.

Young, Alfred F. 2004. *Masquerade: The Life and Times of Deborah Sampson, Continental Soldier.* New York: Knopf.

———. 1993. How radical was the American Revolution? In *Beyond the American Revolution: Explorations in the History of American Radicalism,* ed. Alfred F. Young, 317–64. DeKalb: Northern Illinois University Press. [1981] 1993.

———. 1990. The women of Boston: "Persons of Consequence" in the making of the American Revolution, 1765–76. In *Women and Politics in the Age of Democratic Revolutions,* ed. Harriet B. Applewhite and Darlene G. Levy, 181–226.

———. George Robert Twelves Hewes (1742–1840): A Boston shoemaker and the memory of the American Revolution. In *In Search of Early America: The William and Mary Quarterly, 1943–1993,* 234–88. Richmond: William Byrd Press.

Index